RADICAL PHILOSOPHY

2.11
Series 2 / Winter 2021

Human species as biopolitical concept	
Étienne Balibar	3
The threshold of fire	
Ahmed Diaa Dardir	13
A Reading of Foucault's *Penal Theories and Institutions*	
Michele Spanò	19
Dossier: Kojève on Europe and the USSR	27
Kojève out of Eurasia	
Trevor Wilson	27
Philosophy and the Communist Party	
Alexandre Kojève	31
Toward an assessment of modernity	
Alexandre Kojève	34
The problem is proletarianisation, not capitalism	
Solange Manche	38
Reviews	51
Aaron Benanav, *Automation and the Future of Work*	
Jason E. Smith, *Smart Machines and Service Work*	
Amelia Horgan	51
Judith Butler, *The Force of Non-Violence*	
Adriana Cavarero, Judith Bulter and Bonnie Honig, *Towards a Feminist Ethics of Nonviolence*	
Elizabeth Frazer and Kimberly Hutchings, *Can Political Violence Ever Be Justified?*	
Alister Wedderburn	56
Katrina Forrester, *In the Shadow of Justice*	
Jonathan Egid	60
Bhandar and Ziadah, eds, *Revolutionary Feminisms*	
Helene Kazan	63
Joseph Pugliese, *Biopolitics of the More-Than-Human*	
Chris Wilbert	67
John Molyneux, *The Dialectics of Art*	
Michael Löwy	70
Avery F. Gordon, *The Hawthorn Archive*	
Elena Loizidou	72
Seb Franklin, *The Digitally Disposed*	
Marc Kohlbry	74
Obituary: Jean-Luc Nancy, 1940-2021	
Joanna Hodge	78

Editorial collective
Claudia Aradau
Brenna Bhandar
Victoria Browne
David Cunningham
Peter Hallward
Stewart Martin
Lucie Mercier
Daniel Nemenyi
Hannah Proctor
Rahul Rao
Martina Tazzioli
Chris Wilbert

Engineers
Daniel Nemenyi
Alex Sassmanshausen

* Creative Commons BY-NC-ND
Radical Philosophy, Winter 2021

ISSN 0300-211X
ISBN 978-1-914099-00-7

Human species as biopolitical concept

Étienne Balibar

I submit that the current situation created by the Covid-19 pandemic and its biopolitical consequences reveals something new in the ontological status of the human species which also involves an anthropological 'revolution'.* This is something more than the fact that the combined tendencies called 'globalisation' (which, regardless of whether we assign them a recent or ancient origin, have clearly crossed a line at the end of the twentieth century) have resulted in relativising frontiers or distances, and subjected all human societies to a single system of economic interdependencies, thus realising something of the Marxian prediction (in the *German Ideology*) that every singular being would relate to every other, when the development of their 'productive forces' has reached 'the stage of totality'.[1] It is also not the same as the fact that environmental consequences of global warming, of industrial waste and consumerist pollutions, plus the destruction of biodiversity are now affecting the whole planet and its populations. Of course the links of the Anthropocene with this type of pandemic do clearly exist. But what I want to discuss is something more directly linked to our self-definition as a 'species', working at a more elementary level.

'Crossing the species barrier', a formula used by epidemiologists to describe a zoonosis possibly transmitted from expatriated bats to human populations by some intermediary 'domestic' vectors, indicates the key determination: on the background of environmental disruption, the biological 'event' at the heart of the crisis connects the human species as such to other living species, which alternatively are contaminated and contaminants. But there is more: as we know, a virus is a *limit-case* in the classification of the living: it is not an organism or even a bacteria, but a sequence of nucleic acid surrounded by proteins, which circulates between organisms and 'infects' cells equipped with a certain genotype in order to 'replicate' itself. Organisms are permanently 'colonised' by a great variety of viruses. The pathological effects (hence the *lethality*) are linked to the fact that a given species (in this case, the human) is not immunised against a virus with which it never had before a permanent contact. And the contact itself is due to the fact that individual organisms (e.g. humans) *meet* each other, i.e. *touch* their fellow humans, *breath* the same air, *live* in the same room or *use* the same objects. This generates an open process of *contagion*, or *dissemination*, which of course is more or less extended and rapid depending on the contagiousness of the virus and the intensity of the intercourse between the 'vectors', i.e. 'us' all, with whom viruses form a kind of *travelling association*.

What I submit is that, in this case, 'humankind' or the human 'species' as an ensemble, in its great majority if not in its totality, becomes materially *unified* in a 'passive' manner. Borrowing a formula from Husserl and Deleuze, I am tempted to speak here of a 'passive synthesis' of the human species.[2] This is a phenomenon of *trans-individuation* of the human, whose specific conditions lie both at the *pre-individual* level of the pathogenic circulation of viruses, which connect bodies and cross every frontier despite the prophylactic obstacles, and at the *supra-individual* level, formed by the 'global' system of production and communications, the *institutional* circulation of persons and things.[3] But to describe the emergence of the 'specific transindividual' as construction of an ontological unity, even if negatively linked to illness and death, would be utterly insufficient. It is equally important to indicate that, right away, the process of unification is also a process of *radical divisions*,

---

* A previous version of this article was given as a lecture at the Centre for Research in Modern European Philosophy (CRMEP) of Kingston University, London, on Thursday 25 February 2021.

which I propose to call 'anthropological fractures', because they generate rifts and oppose the human to the other human within what we may call their common 'species-being' (*Gattungswesen*), an expression borrowed from Feuerbach and the young Marx.[4] This is of course the political dimension that official discourses carefully put aside, or minimise, when they refer to the 'universal' character of the problems created by the pandemic and the crisis, invoking common interests of mankind and the necessity of addressing them in a collective manner, arguing that 'we are all in the same boat'.

It is very important to understand here that the generic unity and the radical division are not independent determinations, they form a unity of opposites in the dialectical sense. The process of unification *intensifies* and *generalises* the fractures, while the fractures emerge as the *concrete modality* in which the unity is realised. Of course this is extremely unstable, both morally and politically. A striking feature of the situation is the *differential vulnerability* of humans with respect to the contamination, mainly related to their various 'anthropological differences' (of race, gender, age, pre-existing pathologies) which intersect with class differences (in terms of jobs, revenues, precariousness, housing, access to medical services, etc.) and global geographic inequalities inherited from the history of colonisation. These differences become actual *cracks*, or they tend to fracture the species into biopolitical 'quasi-races', and they are linked to discriminations when it comes to erecting protections against the contagion or to distribute treatments. But the discriminations do not cancel the unification process, in particular because they do not really *block the contagion*, the transindividual dissemination of the pathogenic element.

Nothing makes this more palpable (and more unacceptable) than the 'cosmopolitical' issue of the distribution of vaccines *equally and globally*, which has been raised by the Director of the World Health Organisation, Dr. Tedros Adhanom Ghebreyesus, who has repeatedly requested that the vaccines now available be quickly transformed into 'generic' drugs, which could be produced everywhere under strict biological control, but completely liberated from the restriction of private licenses (as was partially reached in the treatment of AIDS).[5] There is of course no possibility that this becomes the case any time soon, if there is no mass mobilisation to support it, because of the huge financial interests of pharmaceutical corporations and the fierce geopolitical competition about vaccines among powerful states, East and West. The official motto of the WHO, 'One World, One Health', which we could complete as 'One World, One Health, One Species', appears to us as the symbol of this contradiction.

Let me now come to a more specific question, namely the 'epistemological' issue of the Human Species as a concept which is undergoing a theoretical *mutation*. That this mutation is politically determined and has political implications (cosmopolitical, biopolitical) is not something to be just added at the end, it is coextensive with the whole examination. I will discuss four successive points (incompletely, of course): 1) The traditional dilemma of anthropological philosophy; 2) The 'perspectivist' alternative; 3) Towards a relational understanding of the species-production; 4) Which 'synthesis' of History and Evolution are we looking for?

The traditional dilemma of anthropological philosophy

I begin with the dilemma of anthropology. Antithetic orientations are of course as old as the anthropological discourse itself (I am speaking of the Western tradition), and they exist independent of whether 'anthropology' is considered from a philosophical, theological or scientific point of view. Certain dualisms seem to persist through these transformations. It is interesting, for instance, to see that Tim Ingold, the eminent British anthropologist, in his introductory essay called 'Humanity and Animality' to the *Companion Encyclopedia of Anthropology*, is eager to explain that the single term *species* applied to the human has led to a disastrous confusion between the study of *Homo sapiens*, as an animal species among others (admittedly with unique forms of behaviour), and the study of the *human condition* opposed to animality, with the diversity of its cultures.[6] The name 'human' seems to be located at the intersection of two multiplicities, one external or relational, the other intrinsic and typological. But the *singular collective* that it refers to ought not to be identified using the same terminology ... Applying the rules of logical clarification, we should accordingly distinguish *species* from *condition*, the specificity from the diversity.

I believe that it is more interesting to set up against one another the two great discourses between which the debates about philosophical anthropology found themselves divided (especially in Germany at the turn of the twentieth century), as a kind of 'point of heresy'. I will call the first the 'Kantian' discourse because its main orientations derive from the discovery of what, in *The Order of Things*, Michel Foucault would later call the 'empirical-transcendental doublet'.[7] Conversely, the other discourse derives its postulates from the Darwinian revolution (even if, as we know, some important elements of the modern theory of evolution came from previous naturalists, such as Buffon, choosing 'inter-fecundity' as a criterion of the species level, and the understanding of the process of 'speciation' in terms of variation and natural selection only became coherent after the fusion of Darwinism with Mendelian genetics).

Both discourses involve a definition of the *human species*, although from antithetical points of view. Some problems of terminology ought to be discussed here. Historians of ideas and some anthropologists assume that in every culture there is a 'vulgar' (or common) idea of species, expressed by different words, and a 'scientific' or 'theoretical' one, which must evolve with the progress of knowledge. But this is complicated by the fact that different languages always use several terms to express the unity or uniqueness of mankind, which are never distributed in the same manner. For example, it would be impossible to transfer the common English expression 'the human race' (already used in the seventeenth century)[8] into French, but there are some affinities with the German *das menschliche Geschlecht* (sometimes used by Kant, instead of *die menschliche Gattung*, which is more frequent, and is dominant today in this tradition, for example in Habermas), although it also often means what we call 'sex'...

It is certainly possible to say that the Kantian point of view is *idealistic*, since Kant orientates philosophy, history and 'cosmopolitics' towards an *Idea of Man* (*Idee des Menschen/der Menschheit*), whereas Darwin illustrates a *naturalistic* point of view, incorporating the human in a *genealogy* entirely immanent to the transformations of living organisms ('animals') which he terms a 'descent' (thus causing what Freud will call a 'narcissistic blow' to our sense of uniqueness and predestination). This is true of course, but it is important to immediately add another determination. While both referring to the human as *species*, they characterise the 'species-being' in an antithetical manner: in Kant the human species is not only unique in its kind, it *coincides* with a kind, or it is its own 'kind' (*Gattung*, 'genre'), whereas for Darwin the human is a species like any others, but it has a unique way of being divided into varieties or races.[9]

From the Kantian point of view, which preserves the legacy of Cicero's *societas generis humani*, the species is a *community*, albeit a 'virtual' or 'ideal' one (but which must be conscious of itself, or *represented* to its members). From the Darwinian point of view, the species is a *population* which can be divided into *subpopulations*, because its members need to *adapt* to heterogeneous environments and transfer their adaptation to the next generations (which the modern Darwinism will explain through the replication of the genetic material through sexual reproduction, thus creating within the population over time a 'genetic pool'). On both sides of our 'point of heresy', the *One* and the *Multiple* of the human become articulated in an antithetical manner.

From a Kantian point of view, the One is a transcendental *norm* (or a normative idea), which imposes on each

5

subject (or conscience) an equal respect for all the other humans qua *persons* or *rational beings*, thus making it possible (or, rather, mandatory) to view them as *humans alike*. All the individual differences and what Kant calls the 'characters', classifying the humans in types and groups, particularly racial, ethnic and sexual, are relegated to the realm of the *empirical*, which means that they must become neutralised or abstracted from in the formation of the moral community. But in fact this is not exactly true: for it would be a norm without effectivity, especially in history and legislation. The real articulation is a *conflictual process*, a 'pragmatic' subsumption of the empirical differences under the normative idea, which is essentially an *educational process* – called 'culture', or elsewhere more dialectically the 'unsociable sociability' – taking place at the level of the individual and the species. Here things become a little tricky, because we know (in particular through recent critical work, done by Spivak and others) that in this process the empirical differences are converted into *unequal capacities to realise the proper human*, and even leaves the possibility that some racially inferior humans will never be educated, i.e. will never prove able to *recognise* the idea of the community to which they should belong ...[10]

Things are no less complex from the Darwinian and post-Darwinian point of view, where, as I said, the key category is not *community* but *population*, which seems to be a mere empirical principle of gathering, with statistical connotations. This is not the case, in fact, because there is an immanent 'demographic' connection between the One and its underlying Multiplicity, which is provided by the *genealogical link*, therefore a temporal continuity or *continuation*: the long past (called 'descent' or 'origin', in other terms the result of cumulated variations in the 'type' which have been 'selected') is articulated with the uncertain future (which we can call reproduction or heredity), whereas the present – which in a sense is the 'species' itself, or, as contemporary biologists would prefer to say, the moment of *speciation*, is being suspended between the *production* and the *transformation* of the type – a point of equilibrium stretched over time, as it were. Ideally at least, the human qua species is a moment of equilibrium between the *pre-human* revealed by palaeontology and the unknown *post-human*. To this scheme of temporality, there is a crucial spatial or territorial counterpart, since the condition for variations to become concentrated and exclusively reproducible (creating a 'species frontier', as the great post-Darwinian theorist Ernst Mayr will write) is that a subpopulation is *isolated* within a *closed* territory or habitat, or excluded from other territories.[11] I will have to return to this question of the spatial isolation (or non-isolation) because it is bound to play a crucial role in any attempt at rethinking the question of speciation in *relational* terms (both to the environment and to other species).

Before I leave this comparison, I want to add a philosophical remark. Although its other side is the 'empirical' diversity that needs to be subsumed in a 'cultural' process, the Kantian idea is remarkable for its *self-referential* logic, which means that the (normative) 'idea' is not projected from outside. In that sense the Kantian problematic is completely *secularised*, there is no need (at least no visible need) of a Creator.[12] In other terms, the 'absolute' element without which there is no community of the humans is one that they *find in themselves* through the activity of their reason. However it remains an absolute, therefore an abstraction. This problematic perfectly illustrates a concept of the 'human essence' (*menschliches Wesen*) as it is criticised by Marx in the 6th Thesis on Feuerbach: 'an abstraction *inhabiting* each and every individual', more precisely each and every individual's *representation of the common*.[13] This could be considered a weakness, especially if we take everything that Marx doesn't like as an absurdity ... But it is an idea not so easy to bypass from an *ethical* point of view, especially if we try and associate a notion of *'generic' responsibility* towards the future of the community, or its excluded parts, with our notion of humanity. This is why we find a trace of the Kantian point of view, more insistent than ever, in contemporary ethics which attach the moral imperative to the respect for *the life of others*, or to the valorisation of their 'vulnerability'. But then the question will arise whether and why this valorisation should remain *tautologically* enclosed within the 'frontiers' of the *human species*, and not extend to other beings? This of course has to do with the fact that, as I said, for Kant the human is the only species that *coincides with its own kind* by virtue of its morality and rationality. To cross the frontier, one has to substitute rationality and morality with other criteria of *personhood* (which is very much what contemporary animalists try to do).

Paradoxically, the trace of theology is perhaps more

visible in Darwin, although it is translated in the 'materialist' terms of the *production of the species* that, while emerging from the long history of natural selection, has *acquired unique characters*, in particular intellectual and technical capacities which, for Darwin, are already there in 'savages' and culminate in 'civilisation', whereas our *emotional* dispositions according to him are largely inherited from the 'lower animals'. Darwin does not speak of the *centrality* of man in nature, as the Bible used to, but he writes that 'man in the rudest state in which he now exists is *the most dominant animal* that has ever appeared on this earth'.[14] A materialist equivalent of the idea of creation therefore is the question of the 'production' of these 'intellectual faculties' and 'social habits' whose 'supreme importance' has been 'proven by the final arbitration of the battle for life.'[15] And it is on this point that the post-Darwinians (until today) offer the most diverse combinations of discontinuity within continuity, or chance within determinism ...

The 'perspectivist' alternative from the Amazonas

Before I move to what I perceive to be a tendency of contemporary ecology to displace the question of the species in the direction of a superior ensemble, where ideas of uniqueness and frontiers are reformulated, I want to take a few moments to describe a different kind of alternative emerging from within the anthropological tradition in its postcolonial and poststructuralist orientation, which calls itself the *perspectivist* problematic. I find it crucial as a mediation towards overcoming the anthropocentric teleology and the metaphysics of the species-being which institutes a *mirror-effect* between the singular individual and the singular collective, that we can read both in Kant and Darwin, albeit in inverted form. A long discussion would be necessary, because many authors participate in this movement. The most interesting in my opinion are not Descola or Latour, nor even Haraway, but the Brazilian anthropologist Eduardo Viveiros de Castro.[16] With other contemporary authors, de Castro shares the idea that the dualism of 'nature' and 'culture' is a purely Western, or Eurocentric idea, which has been imposed on other civilisations through the colonial conquests. It entails both the idea that the human species has 'extracted' itself from its participation in exchanges (which can be conflictual, even predatory, but involve reciprocity) with other living species, and the idea that all non-human beings can be used for the satisfaction of human needs without limits (provided it be done in a wise, i.e. calculated or rational manner). He therefore proposes a thought experiment, in which the 'human perspective' on the non-humans is substituted, or confronted with a 'non-human perspective' on the humans, particularly a perspective of the *wild species* for whom autochthonous peoples are co-habitants of the same environment.

Keep in mind that this proposal has a political counterpart, for example in the discourse of Native Americans in the Amazonas, who argue that rivers, mountains, forests are 'persons', not only out of 'animist' convictions, but in order to oppose their 'natural right' to the destructive effects of capitalism, in a reversal of the Marxian 'fetishism', where nature is made of pure 'things', ready for exploitation and commodification.[17] I am interested here in the way in which Viveiros de Castro makes use of the powers of *fiction*. He himself approvingly refers to the *myths* of Indian tribes, as transmitted and glossed by shamans, which narrate and set up the exchange of places between the various 'species': we are distinctly humans but also animals (e.g. predators and prey) in the eyes and the mind of the Jaguar or the Snake. There is here a clear influence of the Deleuzian and Kafkaesque motto of 'becoming other' through metamorphoses. This seems to me to be fairly different from the typologies of alternative 'cosmologies' proposed by other authors, which are in fact completely positivist, comparing 'cultures' as formal systems. De Castro doesn't claim to be 'multiculturalist' but 'multinaturalist'. In de Castro, the recourse to fiction (and myth) is a new moment of what Levi-Strauss had called *le regard éloigné*, or the 'view from afar', except that this 'afar' need not be measured in geographical or cultural distance, it is essentially a question of including in our self-reflection as humans, or as a human species, an *imaginary* critique of the *illusion* of uniqueness that is inherent in the classical anthropologies, or to understand that uniqueness not in terms of its own image, but in terms of its relations to other natural beings, through a kind of 'eidetic variation'.[18] Let us try and see how this could be applied to the interpretation of certain recent trends in the understanding of evolution.

Towards a relational understanding of the species-production

From this vantage point, I suggest that we can try and return to the question of what we call 'human species', not in self-referential terms (even if 'located' in a broad spatial-temporal framework) but in terms of its intrinsic relationality to others and the transformations or evolution of these relations. Such a perspective is clearly involved in the form in which recent ecology has tended to react to the very idea of evolution, by suggesting that *what evolves*, or becomes transformed into different types that form relatively stable (through genetic reproduction) and relatively homogeneous (through isolation) collectivities is not a *single species* (or population with specific characters, sharing a 'genetic pool'), but a *system* or a *complex* which always includes a multiplicity of living forms inhabiting the same environment (with different degrees of 'closure') and contributing to the shaping of this environment through their 'activity' (the effects of their metabolism and behaviour). In other terms, the support of evolution, its *hypokeimenon*, is not and cannot be a single species, it must be the relation itself between species in its unstable composition – I am tempted to say *à la Marx* the '*ensemble* of ecological relations', which includes their 'world' and their interaction with that world. Every evolution in that sense is a 'co-evolution', and every co-evolution is a reciprocal transformation or a *mutual 'adaptation'* of the organisms and their '*milieu*' (which, following Canguilhem, I see no difficulty in calling 'dialectical').[19]

Once again, we have to evoke some difficulties of terminology and translation which can also become conceptual resources. Where the English practically has a single term, 'environment', the French or the German use at least two. I used on purpose the French category 'milieu' – supposedly coined in its biological meaning by Buffon out of an analogy with Newtonian physics – rather than the German category *Umwelt* (different from *Umgebung*) because, although the idea of the 'milieu' clearly involves a teleological correspondence between needs and resources, or activities and effects which can be destructive or regulating, and therefore a dilemma of *adaptation and inadaptation* (which in a sense is biological 'life' itself, but can be extended to 'social life'), it does not involve *intentionality*, or the hermeneutic circularity of defining the *Umwelt* through its *meaning for* the organism (essentially the individual organism, and practically the 'superior' animal or vegetal organism). This can be disputed of course. In any case, what I have in mind is the fact that evolutionary theory no longer locates 'adaptation' (in a utilitarian manner) on the side of the living forms, with the 'environment' playing the role of the deterministic constraint which continuously imposes the 'battle for life', eliminating the 'inadapted' unless they change or leave room for others, but *also* on the side of the environment (which in large part is made of other living beings). The relationship must be *symmetrised*, or it must be understood permanently from a 'double perspective' (at least).

As a consequence, the differential of adaptation-inadaptation is taking place in ecosystems which can be ordered hierarchically along the continuous line of successive inclusions: from the *niche* (which is usually defined for a single species, or even variety, e.g. the European wildcat (*felis silvestris*) or the common rat (*rattus rattus*), to the *habitat* where multiple species (cats and rats) coexist, to the *milieu* where certain conditions for life are regulated (e.g. the savannah, or the rainforest), to the *environment* proper, which includes the physical and geological determinations making life possible, to the *planet*, which is the environment of environments. When we discuss evolutionary processes at this final level, the category *history* (history of life, history of the earth) needs to be introduced, but I will return to this in a minute.

Before I switch to the specific question of the human as a product of its relation to its own milieu, allow me another quick remark. I invoke the category 'co-evolution', but there are multiple forms and degrees of co-evolution, some in which genetic or phenotypic transformations are directly correlative, because certain living species live in symbiosis, others in which the transformations are mediately produced, because species are in a relationship of predation, of mutual support in their reproductive process (Deleuze, as we know, was fascinated by the 'coupling' of the wasp and the orchid, which for him is like an unconscious love affair),[20] others in which the transformations involve changes in the rates of growth or extinction of populations. Ecologists and socio-biologists frequently use the term *community* to describe the system of interdependencies between species or forms of life which subsist in the same habitat, or whose regulated interdependency *reproduces* the possibilities ('services') of their environment. They also use the terms *hierarchy* and *domination* – with clear risks of anthropomorphic projection – to describe the fact that the relations of 'exchange' between species are always *dissymmetric*, like relations of *power*: not only because some organisms are used by others in the great cycle that leads from photosynthesis to consumption of vegetables and animals to decomposition and decay, but because a 'community' in a given milieu involves different processes of 'invasion', 'competition' and, notably, 'extinction'. The history of life in the evolutionary process is the history of productions, or speciations, and extinctions through direct or indirect elimination. The question becomes now: is it possible to extend these categories, with their metaphoric resonances, to the level of the planet, or the environment of environments, and what would be the possible articulation with the *singular* character of the 'domination' of the human species in the history of life, even if we perceive it from a *non-anthropocentric* point of view?

Which 'synthesis' of History and Evolution are we looking for?

As we remember, Darwin called the human 'the most dominant animal', which barely conceals an idea of sovereignty (the species that *dominates all other dominants* themselves), but the kind of 'domination' we have to discuss now is more ambivalent, since it includes the possibility that this domination has *simultaneous effects of construction and destruction*. What I have in mind is the fact that – over something like 70,000 or 100,000 years – the humans (for the sake of simplicity let's call them the human species, *homo sapiens sapiens*), eliminating or mixing with some other humans, have expanded their 'habitat' from a limited region in the African high plains to the whole planet, so that in fact there is practically no *particular milieu* for the human species, or there is a *quasi-universal milieu*: only very few regions in the globe today are not 'inhabited', and in fact they are all *exploited*, with global warming helping to cross the last frontiers.

If we remember Ernst Mayr's theory of territorial isolation as a condition for the emergence of new species and his concept of the 'species frontier', we may suggest the following model, which is paradoxical only in appearance: through the progressive displacement and removal of frontiers, the human species has generated for itself (and, as a consequence, also for many others) a process of *de-isolation* (of course there have been more complex cycles of partial isolation and reconvening) which makes it impossible for the species to *evolve* in the traditional sense, or along the purely Darwinian mechanism of variation plus natural selection. As the human species 'colonised' the planet and therefore, in the end, produced a global environment where its own activities (agricultural, industrial) *modify the conditions of variation and selection for all other species*, which also before our eyes leads to a massive *extinction* of other species (called by Elizabeth Kolbert and others the 'sixth mass extinction in the history of life'),[21] the 'domination' of the human (or the 'becoming dominant' of the human as a species in the totality of environments) may be said to have transformed not the 'laws' of evolution, but certainly its *conditions*, and therefore its *tendencies*. I would also risk the formulation, which returns us to the immediate present: the human species has practically 'crossed' every species barrier technically or biologically, but, in 'doing' this – if it is a 'deed' – it has created the conditions for its *own 'barrier' as a species* to be crossed by certain organisms or quasi-organisms (such as viruses), erecting protections which are continuously got around (or, in the terminology of Jacques Derrida and Roberto Esposito, creating immunities which become auto-immunities).[22]

Apparently, 'dominance' in the ecological sense is itself symmetric, or it is intrinsically fragile and ambivalent in the long run. However, is it satisfactory to say that the human species has made it possible for itself *not to evolve*? Shouldn't we rather change our perspective and consider the question from the relational angle of mutual adaptation? What I have described in broad terms is a process of transformation of the world, which can be called a *colonisation* (and I am fully aware of the problems which this category will raise when we compare it to the *historical and political* meaning of the idea of colonisation). I have described the human species as the *colonising species* in the co-evolution of life and environment. How to imagine that this would not affect the definition of the human *as a species* in return? It would be a complete non-sense with respect to our premises ... In fact, the human species is not only colonising territories and using their resources in multiple manners which are unequally creative or destructive, it is *colonising itself*, or *self-colonising*, both extensively in terms of including human populations within the realm of its expansions (a process which culminates in the 'proper' colonisation of the modern era, driven by capitalism and other interests or 'missions'), and intensively in the form of the permanent destruction and reconstruction of its own habitats everywhere (think of Habermas's 'colonisation of the life world').[23] But this consideration leads to a more general, and also more problematic one: namely the idea that we cannot circumscribe our understanding of the idea of speciation and evolution as 'production' of a species-type with the limited criterion of a genetic determination (and genetic material or 'pool'), however important this is (all the more when it becomes possible to *technically* modify the genetic material for medical or eugenic purposes). In the case of the human, and as a direct counterpart to its 'domination' of the universal milieu, there is a kind of *reflexive* or *endogenous* evolution, which at the same time *extracts* the human from the 'community' of which it is part, and provides it with increasingly more efficient means of transformation – which however are never able to anticipate and master their own consequences. This is not a zero-sum game, in which nature becomes 'weaker' and 'subservient' as man, its alleged 'master and possessor', has become stronger and 'dominant'. As Spinoza had already written in the single axiom of his *Ethics*, part IV: 'There is no singular thing in Nature than which there is not another more powerful and stronger. Whatever one is given, there is another more powerful by which the first can be destroyed'; which we could translate as: 'the stronger or more effective man becomes in nature, the stronger and even more effective nature proves to be.'[24]

More speculatively: as we try and understand what kind of *new species* the human has become as a consequence of its own history, we must also elaborate a *new concept of species*. This makes us think of what is commonly called the 'reversing effect of culture' on 'nature' itself in the case of man, or the emergence of a 'second nature' which substitutes the 'first' (not only for the human, but for its others as well). This is a long and fascinating history of philosophical ideas indeed ... However I would prefer to follow the more concrete path already indicated with the idea of the colonising and self-colonising species. This is certainly a decisive criterion, but probably not the only one, or one that does not operate *alone*.

In my recent readings and ruminations, I have come to the idea that two other characteristics are equally important, and complementary. Firstly, there is the character of *domestication*, because the humans are the only 'domesticating' and 'self-domesticating' species, thus introducing *among the living beings* an increasingly decisive cleavage between two categories: the 'wild', or simply *non-domesticated* species, and the 'companion species' (as Donna Haraway calls them),[25] i.e. the domesticated species in various manners and enclosures, creating for themselves a 'niche' among their domestic animals. And then there is the character of the *artificialisation* of life, because the human is the only species which, extracting materials and instruments from its own environment, is able to create a complete system of *prosthetic supplements* without which no individual can exist – not even one minute – between birth and death, 'externalising' the biological, intellectual, affective conditions of its own life, or developing an 'external body': what Bernard Stiegler, developing suggestions from the great prehistorian and archaeologist André Leroi-Gourhan, had called 'exosomatisation'.[26]

While colonisation and self-colonisation 'territorialise' the human species in a process of determined negation of all pre-existing territorial boundaries, domestication and self-domestication decisively *displace the frontier* between the human and the non-human, making it possible for the humans to live and inhabit more or less symbiotically among an increasing proportion of non-humans (animals or plants), but also installing these non-humans *on the side of the human* in the great divide (we might ask after De Castro what certainly makes the perception of humans as animals so widely different for a jaguar and a milking cow?), until domestication itself is superseded by industrial agriculture and the biochemical production of food. And *artificialisation* is an extremely powerful vector of *transindividuality*, since the 'external body' is never purely personal, or individual, it is made of connected systems, shared by many at the same time. Marx had a glimpse of that with his 'general intellect'.[27] All these determinations – colonisation, domestication, artificialisation – are of course aspects of what used to be called 'socialisation', seen from an evolutionary standpoint. Which calls for a careful discussion.

Only now therefore have I arrived at the point where I could raise my last questions, but I am already beyond the limits of time. I will therefore content myself with *naming* the two questions which are inevitable. In fact they are correlative.

The first is the following: how do we articulate the concepts of *evolution* and *history*? Clearly, there is a question of regimes of temporality here as well as of ontological support. In his celebrated essay *The Climate of History: Four Theses* from 2009, Dipesh Chakrabarty has proposed to draw the consequences of the 'Anthropocene' by *merging* or re-connecting geological time and social time, which he considers two varieties of history.[28] The problem I want to raise now with respect to 'evolution' and 'history' is similar, perhaps it is even another dimension of the same, but it raises quite different questions and aporias. I see it as an absolute precondition for the investigation of the problem that we resolutely abandon every anthropocentrism on the side of evolution and we completely eliminate 'evolutionism' on the side of history (which was certainly not the case in any of the great philosophies of history, including Marxism). We need to construct a reciprocity, understand what kind of evolution in the anthropological sense is taking place *within history*, how historical processes *transform the species-being*, but also conversely what kind of history has *modified the course of evolution*, both for man and for the other components of the 'living community'.

At this point the question of capitalism arises, inevitably. I am completely aware of the fact that my readers here (as on some previous occasions) could be very surprised. They want to ask: what role does capitalism play in your description of the transformation of the environment and the abolition of species barriers (or frontiers)? And perhaps: how dare you inscribe processes of artificialisation, domestication, and above all colonisation, in a process of historical evolution whose 'subject', both patient and agent, would be this 'abstraction', the human species, never mentioning or apparently marginalising the *capitalist* determination of this process?

My tentative answer is twofold. First, *this is not an abstraction*, this is the *concrete* process of the *becoming species* of the human, its *Gattungswerden*, which began long before capitalism, although we observe its completion, or 'passive synthesis', only now. Second, in this history, capitalism is not marginal, or secondary, far from it. The reference to capitalism is absolutely crucial if we want to avoid the illusion of retrospective *necessity* (precisely what an evolutionist view of capitalism did not escape). Capitalism did not only change the course of history, it *changed the course of evolution*. If the emergence of the human species is the 'catastrophe', in the topological sense,[29] within the evolution of life and the planet, capitalism is the 'catastrophe' within this catastrophe: it is the social and economic mutation that dramatically *accelerates* and probably *bifurcates* within the processes of colonisation, domestication and artificialisation. The anthropology of *homo capitalisticus* is certainly not inexistent, but barely sufficient already to completely understand our present. It should be considered one of our main philosophical tasks.

Étienne Balibar is Anniversary Chair Professor at the Centre for Research in Modern European Philosophy (CRMEP) at Kingston University and a Visiting Professor at the Department of French and Romance Philology at Columbia University.

Notes

1. Karl Marx (with Friedrich Engels and Moses Hess), *The German Ideology* (1845; first publication 1930): 'Thus things have now come to such a pass that the individuals must appropriate the existing totality of productive forces, not only to achieve self-activity, but, also, merely to safeguard their very existence. This appropriation is first determined by the object to be appropriated, the productive forces, which have been developed to a totality and which only exist within a universal intercourse. From this aspect alone, therefore, this appropriation must have a universal character corresponding to the productive forces and the intercourse.' https://www.marxists.org/archive/marx/

works/1845/german-ideology/ch01d.htm.

2. In the philosophy of Edmund Husserl a 'passive synthesis' (of the transcendental subject) is a process of cultural experience without reflection or intention that 'accumulates' meanings preparing the emergence of consciousness (see *Cartesian Meditations*, 1929, IV). Deleuze adopted the notion to give it a vast application in *Difference and Repetition* (1969) where it connotes, in particular, the 'correspondences' between series or multiplicities which make an experience of time possible.

3. The concept 'transindividual' was introduced in the mid-twentieth century by Jacques Lacan, Lucien Goldman, and especially Gilbert Simondon. I have used it to relate a group of philosophers who simultaneously reject 'individualism' and 'holism' in philosophy and politics (Spinoza, Marx, Freud). See my book *Spinoza, the Transindividual*, trans. Mark G. E. Kelly (Edinburgh: Edinburgh University Press 2020); also Jason Read, *The Politics of Transindividuality* (Leiden: Brill 2016).

4. See Luca Basso: *Marx and Singularity. From the Early Writings to the Grundrisse*, trans. Arianna Bove (Leiden: Brill 2012), ch. 1.

5. See his declarations: Tedros Adhanom Ghebreyesus, 'Vaccine Nationalism Harms Everyone and Protects No One', *Foreign Policy*, 2 February 2021, https://foreignpolicy.com/2021/02/02/vaccine-nationalism-harms-everyone-and-protects-no-one.

6. Tim Ingold, ed., *Companion Encyclopedia of Anthropology: Humanity, Culture and Social Life* (London and New York: Routledge, 2002).

7. Michel Foucault, *The Order of Things: An Archaeology of the Human Sciences* (London and New York: Routledge, 2002); see my commentary 'Foucault's Point of Heresy: "Quasi-Transcendentals" and the Transdisciplinary Function of the Episteme', *Theory, Culture & Society* 32:5-6 (2015), 45–77.

8. The *Oxford English Dictionary* gives the following example: 'Whatever the cause of our different colour be, I'm sure we're all of human Race.' (C. Gildon *Post-boy rob'd of his Mail* I. xlv. 148 (1692)) in 'human, adj. and n.' OED online. September 2021, Oxford University Press, https://www.oed.com/view/Entry/89262

9. Immanuel Kant, *Groundwork of the Metaphysics of Morals*, ed. and trans. Mary Gregor (Cambridge: Cambridge University Press 1997); Charles Darwin, *The Descent of Man, and Selection in Relation to Sex* (London: John Murray, 1906).

10. Gayatri Chakravorty Spivak, *A Critique of Postcolonial Reason: Towards a History of the Vanishing Present* (Cambridge, MA and London: Harvard University Press, 1999). I am also relying on the recent PhD thesis by Marie Louise Krogh at Kingston University: *Territory and Temporality: The Geopolitical Imaginary of German Philosophies of History* (2020).

11. Ernst Mayr, *Population, Species and Evolution* (Cambridge, MA and London: Harvard University Press, 1970).

12. As we know in Kant 'God' becomes a moral idea (which he calls a 'postulate of practical reason'), located not at the *origin* but at the (hypothetic) *end* of history.

13. See my commentary 'From Philosophical Anthropology to Social Ontology and Back: What to Do with Marx's Sixth Thesis on Feuerbach?', *Postmodern Culture* 22:3 (2012).

14. Darwin, *The Descent of Man*, Part I, chapter II. On the intrinsic tension between secularism and theology in Darwin's philosophy (therefore scientific thinking), see Dominique Lecourt, *L'Amérique entre la Bible et Darwin* (Paris: Presses Universitaires de France, 1992).

15. Ibid.

16. Eduardo Viveiros de Castro, *Cannibal Metaphysics*, ed. and trans. Peter Skafish (Minneapolis: Univocal 2014); see also 'Cosmological Deixis and Amerindian Perspectivism', *The Journal of the Royal Anthropological Institute* 4:3 (1998).

17. See Ailton Krenak, *Idées pour retarder la fin du monde*, postface by Eduardo Viveiros de Castro, trans. Julien Pallotta (Bellevaux: Editions Dehors 2020).

18. Claude Levi Strauss, *The View from Afar*, trans. Joachim Neugroschel and Phoebe Hoss (Chicago: University of Chicago Press 1985).

19. Georges Canguilhem, 'Le vivant et son milieu', in *La connaissance de la vie*, 2nd edition (Paris: Vrin, 1965); *Knowledge of Life*, eds. Paola Marrati and Todd Meyers, trans. Stefanos Geroulanos and Daniela Ginsburg (New York: Fordham University Press, 2008).

20. See Gilles Deleuze and Félix Guattari, *A Thousand Plateaus Capitalism and Schizophrenia II*, trans. Brian Massumi (Minneapolis: University of Minnesota Press 1987), ch 10.

21. Elizabeth Kolbert, *The Sixth Extinction: An Unnatural History* (London and New York: Bloomsbury Press, 2015).

22. Jacques Derrida, *Rogues: Two Essays on Reason* (Standford: Stanford University Press, 2005); Roberto Esposito, *Immunitas: The Protection and Negation of Life* (Cambridge: Polity Press 2011).

23. Jürgen Habermas, *The Theory of Communicative Action, vol.2 : Lifeworld and system: a critique of functionalist reason*, trans. Thomas MacCarthy (Boston: Beacon Press, 1985).

24. See Benedictus de Spinoza, *The Ethics*, trans. Edwin Curley, in *The Collected Works of Spinoza*, vol. 1 (Princeton: Princeton University Press, 1985).

25. Donna Haraway, *The Companion Species Manifesto: Dogs, People, and Significant Otherness* (Chicago: Prickly Paradigm Press, 2003).

26. Bernard Stiegler & The Collectif Internatio, eds, *Bifurquer. Il n'y a pas d'alternative* (Paris: les Liens qui libèrent, 2020); see also https://www.lesauterhin.eu/a-propos-de-bifurquer-2-anthropocene-exosomatisation-et-neguentropie/

27. Karl Marx, *The Grundrisse*, trans. Martin Nicolaus. (London: Penguin Books & New Left Review, 1973), Notebook VII, 'Fixed capital and circulating capital as two particular kinds of capital. Fixed capital and continuity of the production process. – Machinery and living labour. (Business of inventing)', https://www.marxists.org/archive/marx/-works/1857/grundrisse/ch14.htm

28. Now included and expanded in Dipesh Chakrabarty, *The Climate of History in a Planetary Age* (Chicago: University of Chicago Press, 2021).

29. 'Topological' refers here to the mathematical 'theory of catastrophes'. See René Thom, *Structural Stability and Morphogenesis*, trans. David H. Fowler (Reading, MA: W. A. Benjamin, 1975).

The threshold of fire
Man the shooter and his subhuman incendiary Other
Ahmed Diaa Dardir

The white gunman and the 'rioters, anarchists, arsonists and flag-burners'

On 25 August 2020, seventeen-year-old (white) Kyle Rittenhouse shot three antiracist protesters in the US state of Wisconsin, killing two and seriously injuring the third. Equally shocking was the impunity with which the shooting was carried out.* Rittenhouse was protected by the police from the angry crowd eager to enact street justice against their assailant; he was then given a bottle of water and released. It was only the next day that Rittenhouse, convinced he was not guilty of murder, handed himself in to the authorities of a different state. His claim that he opened fire 'to protect business and people' (in this order) gained currency among many in the US. Whereas the right-wing hailed him as a hero, mainstream liberals accepted the moral relativism and two sidedness of the situation, especially as the image of the gun-wielding Rittenhouse (among other white supremacist armed militias, euphemised as vigilantes) was constructed against the image of a rioting, sabotaging and arsonist mob as a threat to 'business and people'. *ABC News*, for example, presented the incident as a matter of debate. Providing the assailant with a justified motive (he 'joined several other armed people in the streets of Kenosha, where businesses had been vandalized and buildings burned following a police shooting that left … a Black man paralyzed'), it presented the two sides of the 'debate' as equally valid while disproportionately privileging the pro-shooting narrative, at least in terms of length:

To some, Rittenhouse is a domestic terrorist whose very presence with a rifle incited the protesters. But to others – who have become frustrated with demonstrations and unrest across the country – he's seen as a hero who took up arms to protect people who were left unprotected.

'Kyle is an innocent boy who justifiably exercised his fundamental right of self-defense. In doing so, he likely saved his own life and possibly the lives of others', said Lin Wood, a prominent Atlanta attorney who is now part of a team representing Rittenhouse.[1]

The incident is a microcosm of the larger confrontation. The recent uprising was incited by the targeted killing of African Americans by police forces, parastate militias and property-owning white citizens 'standing their ground'. The Black Lives Matter movement, the black and/or multi-ethnic dissident crowd, the left, Antifa or the protesters more broadly appear on the other hand as bearing incendiary and licentious forms of fire that burn property, indiscriminately threaten people, act as a vehicle and/or cover-up for looting and may go as far as desecrating the white man's most sacred symbol: the US flag. They are, in the words of former US President Donald Trump, 'rioters, anarchists, arsonists and flag-burners'.[2] Even when no shooting is involved the dichotomy is still present, as right-wing groups organise armed rallies, whereas antiracism protests are depicted as engaging in various forms of riot, vandalism and incendiarism.

Two types of fire thus emerge and set the parameters for this confrontation. One is regimented in firearms, wielded by institutions and militias that are predominantly white and targeted against protesters and African

---

* Thanks to Dina Fergani and Hanine Hassan for commenting on earlier versions of this paper, and to Joseph Massad for his continued support.

Americans, thus metonymising the white man, his right to bear arms, his state and its/their military and paramilitary organisations, his prerogative to 'protect' and ultimately exert his mastery, through fire, over other members of the population. The second is incendiary fire, the random fire of arsonists, looters and rioters, the metonym for the incendiary crowd and its chaotic and destructive rebellion. The hierarchised typology that privileges aimed and ostensibly precise gunfire over licentious arson, produces a hierarchisation of its bearers, placing the white man's others at the threshold of fire and civilisation.

The following account situates this hierarchisation within the colonial history of typifying fire. Since the nineteenth century, fire has operated as a civilisational threshold in Western political thought. Imagined as man's first invention and operating within an epistemic regime of evolutionism, the ability to ignite, wield, control and use fire separates humans from other creatures. The differential typology of fire nevertheless goes further. At the threshold of fire stand subhuman forms that are stuck between animality and humanity, namely primitive savages, children (or in some representations, adolescents) and women (the study of the relationship between fire and femininity, between incendiarism and hysteria, requires a different archive and a different set of tools, and will therefore not form part of this essay). Stuck at the threshold of fire, these subhuman forms were able to ignite and wield fire, and in some cases wield lesser forms of fire power, but lacked mastery and restraint. This typology will translate later into the opposition between, on the one side, the self-detonating body of the misfiring terrorist, and on the other, the precise, targeted, laser-guided, smart and tactical weaponry of the white man and his superpower. For reasons of space, before we return to the contemporary US in conclusion, my analysis will home in on a set of archival and literary representations of emblematic colonial encounters around fire while drawing parallels with counterrevolution/counterinsurgency in Europe and the US.

Fire, revolution and the primitive

In 1882, during the British invasion of Egypt and after three days of British bombardment, fire spread through many neighbourhoods of the city of Alexandria. It was unthinkable, however, for the British press as well as many Arab news outlets, that the conflagration had been caused by British gunfire.[3] On the contrary, the fire had to have been the work of indigenous *incendiaries*. Perhaps for the British media the double meaning of the term made it suitable for denoting incendiarism qua arson and incendiarism qua subversive political activities.[4] This incendiarism and arson, furthermore, could not have served any strategic purpose according to the prevalent representations of the event, which either depicted the

9738—Interior of Old Egyptian Fort, Destroyed by English Fleet, July 1882, Alexandria, Egypt.

indigenous rebels as an amorphous crowd emitting noise and spreading chaos and fire,[5] or their leaders as pyromaniacs who ordered the arson[6] and showed nothing but satisfaction when receiving news of the burning down of their city.[7]

When Ahmad 'Urabi, the rebel leader, was brought to trial, his claims that Alexandria caught fire as a result of the British bombardment were dismissed as nonsensical and *childish*.[8] In opposition to the pyromaniac Egyptian rebels, pro-British discourse seems to have endowed British missiles with rational faculties that were denied to indigenous subjects. Salim al-Naqqash, the pro-British Syrian-Alexandrian chronicler of the events of the invasion, recorded a few incidents in which British missiles did in fact fall into residential quarters, but found their way to uninhabited chambers and sat there quietly without exploding.[9] Salim Faris al-Shidyaq, another pro-British author running one of the most influential pan-Arab newspapers of the time, *al-Jawa'ib*, while conceding that part of the conflagration may have been caused by British bombardment (a concession he would later retract with the defeat of 'Urabi), expressed his wish that the British might have bombed the city 'in a manner that caused no harm'.[10] Even when reprimanding the British for their bombardment, these authors endowed their fire with purpose: they had the right to bomb the city but not to cause harm; their bombs did show / could have shown restraint and spared civilian targets.

Two themes emerge in these representations. The first is of a purposeful bombardment that causes no fire, or at least nothing more than the strategic surgical fire it aims to ignite or, in the worst case, could potentially have not caused harm where it did (as per al-Shidyaq's fantasy). The second is of a set of politically subversive activities that spread uncontrolled and purposeless fire.[11] These themes are underlined by two intersecting though not identical biases. First, there is a clear statist bias. The fire of *order* is similarly orderly.[12] Even when belligerent, it hits its intended targets precisely, refrains from exploding in the midst of civilian targets and acts as the agent of order and discipline. The fire of the rebels, on the other hand, is an *incendiary* agent that causes a random and purposeless conflagration with no aim other than arson itself. This theme was consecrated a decade earlier during the Paris Commune, when the fire that consumed many of Paris's monumental governmental buildings after over a month of bombardment by the government in Versailles, and during the exchange of fire between the invading forces of *order* and the retreating revolutionary forces, was attributed to a fit of hysterical incendiarism with which the rebels – especially the women amongst them – were afflicted. Indeed, accounts in the English, French and Arabic press explicitly and implicitly compared 'Urabi and his comrades to the communards,[13] and al-Shidyaq went as far as attributing the fire of Alexandria to the work of former communards who had found their way into the ranks of 'Urabi.[14]

Second, there is the civilisational and racial bias. Fire and more specifically wild and incendiary fire, fire not regimented in firearms or combustion engines, represents a reversion to nature that is opposed, according to the dogmas of modernity, to civilisation. In representations of the Commune, this regression to incendiary barbarism was indeed expressed through the likening of the Parisian revolutionaries and their sympathisers to 'barbarians', 'heathens', 'negro kings' and a whole litany of Europe's others.[15] In representations of the British invasion of Egypt, this civilisational bias dominates the narrative and appears in the form of a racialised dialectic of mastery and non-mastery. Whereas the white man controlled fire and used it as an orderly civilising force, the indigenous Egyptian was depicted as unable to use this technology. Opposed to the occupiers' tactical, precise and sometimes 'lively'[16] fire, and side by side with the natives' incendiary, arsonist, always destructive but never tactical fire, the Egyptians were frequently depicted as bludgeoning, clubbing, stabbing, ripping apart and stoning the foreigners, but seldom as shooting at them. This is especially evident in the extended report compiled by the British Foreign Office laying out the putative details of the events in Alexandria during the invasion, in which images of violence perpetrated by the natives with sticks, cold weapons and bare hands are repeated ad nauseam, while incidents of natives using gunfire against their occupiers are surprisingly scarce – more surprising once we take into account that the people's movement against the occupiers was sparked and supported by the Egyptian army. Even when the natives appear armed, according to this report, and even when Egyptian army soldiers are part of the confrontation, they use the bayonets of their guns to stab the foreigners, instead of using the guns to shoot,[17] as if this wondrous technology was beyond their comprehension. Two decades later, an Egyptian nationalist newspaper, *al-Liwa'*, used these inconsistencies to question the whole narrative of indigenous hatred and violence against the foreigners, wondering why, if the Alexandrian natives had been as hateful and fanatical as the reports made them out to be, they only used sticks and bayonets and refrained from using firearms.[18]

Instead of attempting to resolve, verify or dismiss these inconsistencies, I read them as symptoms of a civilisational-racial bias, a civilisational teleology of wielding and mastering fire, which puts sophisticated, tactical and lively (gun)fire in the hands of the European, leaving the non-European at a stage of non-mastery, marvelling at, misusing and perverting the wondrous (Western) technologies of fire and guns.[19] A few years later, as another wave of anticolonial protests (dubbed the 1919 revolt/revolution) swept the country, the appearance of armed resistance perplexed British Intelligence, which ventured that Egyptian partisans must have acquired their weapons through Greek and Armenian proxies.[20] It is as if firearms needed to pass down a racial-civilisational scale, from the hands of white Europeans to the hands of lesser Europeans (or Asians – literally Caucasian, even beyond the myth of a Caucasian race – who are Europeanised through their Christianity, their light complexion and their historical ties to Europe's forerunner, Christendom, in the case of Armenians) and finally to the hands of the African/Arab natives. This hierarchisation of fire and its users is also ontogenetic. Natives who are subjected to colonialism's civilising mission emerge as infantile and childish (the same term that was used by *al-Jawa'ib* to describe 'Urabi). They need to learn the proper handling of fire as part of their colonial education. This narrativisation of the typologies and threshold of fire within the ontogenetic and phylogenetic teleologies of colonialism's civilising mission is still more evident, as I am about to show, in the literary fiction of British but also US empire.

The adolescent and the savage

Present since the dawn of the literary fantasies of the British Empire,[21] the threshold of fire marked the colonial experience beyond the context of Egypt and beyond the British Empire. Around the same time that the aforementioned confrontations were transpiring in Egypt, Rudyard Kipling – literary spokesperson of the British Empire and of Western Imperialism more broadly – was narrativising this threshold of fire to usher Mowgli, the man-cub raised in the forest, into civilisation and manhood in *The Jungle Book*. Mowgli's entry into manhood is narrativised as an ascent through the differential grid of fire, from blazing torch to hunter's gun and from unwitting arson to purposeful and aimed gunfire. The ability to wield fire, which Mowgli steals from the 'man village', marks his separation from the jungle, his mastery over other creatures, and his subsequent path to manhood. (The jungle itself signifies both the state of nature the civilised man needs to break with, and the infancy the adult man needs to leave behind: as Kipling urges his reader, 'Take up the White Man's burden / Have done with childish days'.) This narrativisation of fire, presented in the first episode of *The Jungle Book*, is more than preserved in the two popular Walt Disney cinematic adaptations of the book: it becomes the overarching theme and dominant plot line in the 1967 and especially the 2016 films.

The centrality of the threshold of fire across the three versions of *The Jungle Book* highlights its salience not only across times but also across empires. No author represents the cultural and literary apparatus of empire better than Rudyard Kipling. A British colonial born in India who went on to write about the country with Orientalist flair and to support British colonial designs in and beyond his birthplace, his literary support for empire went beyond his allegiance to Britain. Kipling is remembered as much for his famous poetic apology for US imperialism – 'The White Man's Burden' – which may also be read as a paean to Western imperialism as such. Similarly, no medium represents the ideological appeal of the US empire and its hold over the hearts and minds of children across the globe better than Walt Disney movies. The hierarchised typology of fire is not exclusive to British imperialist literature, *The Jungle Book*, or even the realm of literary and cinematic fiction. As I noted in the introduction, it is also evident in the opposition between the explosive, out of control fire of the racialised terrorist and the tactical, strategic, surgical, smart, (computer and/or laser) guided or otherwise friendly fire of Western superpowers – not to mention in racial confrontations in and beyond the contemporary US.

The Jungle Book nevertheless serves to highlight how this typology of fire positions both the primitive and the adolescent at a liminal stage between animal and man. This liminality is exemplified by Mowgli (in Kipling's text and in the 2016 film adaptation, which alludes unmistakably to puberty) whose handling of fire passes through a stage of delirium and lack of restraint. In the original text he threatens the inhabitants of the jungle including the pack of wolves to which he previously belonged; in the 2016 film he sets the whole jungle ablaze. Newly inaugurated into humanity, like savages and adolescents, but unlike the white colonial, Mowgli is yet to learn 'To veil the threat of terror / And check the show of pride'.[22]

Mowgli is expected to transcend this unfortunate but necessary stage of misfire. Indeed Mowgli's words during his fire-frenzy, in Kipling's original text, carry within them the prophecy that after becoming a man and breaking with the jungle, he will return as a hunter. This once more recalls the recent conflagrations in the US, where the teenage Rittenhouse exercises his white male prerogative to handle fire, but like Mowgli, fires carelessly and prematurely. Part of the controversy surrounding Rittenhouse centred on the fact that he was a year younger than the legal age for openly carrying a gun.

The threshold of fire

In the US, both the young militiaman and the radical (ethnically diverse and/or predominantly black) crowd stand at the threshold of fire. The former is expected to train to go beyond this threshold, to learn not to fire prematurely or openly when the media is watching, to put fire to good use in colonial and disciplinary endeavours,[23] 'to veil the threat of terror / And check the show of pride'. The latter, so long as they refuse to enlist in the disciplinary and repressive institutions of US empire or the paramilitary organisations of white nationalism, are doomed to remain stuck at the threshold of the fire which they ultimately pervert: their action is always understood as vandalism and incendiarism and their organisation as open terror.

This confrontation continually produces gunfire as the white man's domain, allowing him the privilege of staging armed rallies and mass shootings. It is telling that Rittenhouse's legal defence team plans to plead the legality of the shooting and killing on the grounds that Rittenhouse was acting as part of an organised militia, a right that the US Constitution grants its white and white supremacist subjects, at least in right-wing interpretations of it.[24] It is also worth noting how the gun lobby in the US, including the National Rifle Association, refuses to recognise that the enjoyment of this right might extend beyond its privileged white bearers, as when the Black Panther Party claimed the right to bear arms in its capacity as an organised militia. This defence gains special significance against the allegation that Rittenhouse's victims were also armed. The black mob is armed haphazardly, the white man is armed as part of an organised militia. The black mob shoots randomly,[25] the white man aims and shoots carefully, to kill if necessary. The black mob's random firing may cause terror, but the white man eventually dominates through his precise, if at times premature, firing.

Ahmed Dardir is a visiting fellow at the Cairo Institute for Liberal Arts and Sciences.

Notes

1. Stephen Groves and Bernard Condon, 'Teen accused of killing 2 thrust into debate over protests', *ABC News*, 29 August 2020.
2. Mario Koran, '"He's paying attention to people like us": Trump's message finds fans in Wisconsin', *The Guardian*, 18 September 2020.
3. UK Foreign Office, 'Correspondences Respecting the Riots at Alexandria on the 11th June 1882', the National Archives, UK, FO 881/4741. See also Salim al-Naqqash, *Misr lil-Misriyyin* [Egypt for the Egyptians], vol. 5 (Alexandria: Matba'at al-Mahrusah, 1884), which provides the first (and perhaps only) chronicling of the events of the invasion in Arabic and which relies almost exclusively on British and pro-British reports.
4. For example 'England and Egypt: Arrival of Reinforcements; The Intervention Question; Statement of French Policy', *The Standard*, 18 July 1882, 5 and 'The Campaign in Egypt: Sirg. Wolseley At Ramleh; A Proclamation to the Egyptians; Fire at Alexandria', *The Standard*, 17 August 1882, 5.
5. Al-Naqqash, *Misr lil Misriyyin*, 140–142; UK Foreign Office, 'Correspondences Respecting the Riots', 1; 'Outbreak in Egypt: Rioting in Alexandria; Attack on Europeans; the British Consul Wounded', *The Standard*, 12 June 1882, 5.
6. Salim Faris al-Shidyaq, 'khitam al-mas'alah al misriyyah' ['Conclusion to the Egyptian Question'], *Al-Jawa'ib*, 7 Dhu al-Qidah 1299 (19 September 1882).
7. Salim Faris al-Shidyaq, 'muhakamat 'urabi' ['Urabi's trial'], *Al-Jawa'ib*, 2 Safar 1300 (12 December 1882), 1.
8. Ibid.
9. Al-Naqqash, *Misr lil Misriyyin*, 90.
10. Salim Faris al-Shidyaq, 'al-ahwal al-hadirah wa al-mas'alah

al-misriyyah' ['Current affairs and the Egyptian question'], *Al-Jawa'ib*, 3 Ramadan 1299 (19 July 1882), 1.

11. This is evident in terms such as 'mutineers', which *The Standard* used to describe the indigenous crowd, and 'anarchy', which it used to denote their activities and effects. See 'Affairs in Egypt (from our correspondent)', *The Standard*, 7 January 1882, 5; 'The State of Egypt: Debate in the French Chamber; The Movements of Arabi [sic]; Conditions of Alexandria', 19 July 1882, 5; 27 July 1882, 4.

12. See how the British forces are depicted as attempting to extinguish the fire spread by the native crowd and how the local authorities are depicted as failing or refusing to extinguish the fire or curb the incendiarism in 'England and Egypt', 5 and 'The Campaign in Egypt', 5.

13. Ahmed Dardir, *Licentious Topographies: Space and the Traumas of Colonial Subjectivity in Modern Egypt*, Doctoral Dissertation, Columbia University, New York, 2018, 302–308.

14. al-Shidyaq, 'khitam', 1.

15. 'The Fighting in Paris', *The Standard*, 29 May 1871, 4; see also Janet Beizer, *Ventriloquized Bodies: Narratives of Hysteria in Nineteenth-Century France* (Ithaca: Cornell University Press, 1994), 217.

16. UK Foreign Office, 'Correspondences Respecting the Riots', 1.

17. Ibid., 1, 62.

18. Mustafa Kamil, 'hadith al-Iskandariyyah' ['The Alexandria Incident'], *Al-Liwa'*, 11 August 1901, 1.

19. Notwithstanding, of course, that gunpowder is a Chinese invention which was known to the Arabs before it entered Europe. What we are interested here is the mythistory of progress rather than the actual history of scientific discovery.

20. 'Intelligence reports and notes on the political background to the nationalist riots of 1919 by Colonel F H Smith', the National Archives, UK, FO 141/753/6.

21. See for example how fire appears in Daniel Defoe's *Robinson Crusoe* as one of Crusoe's prerogatives, something he chooses to bestow on Friday as part of his colonial education.

22. Rudyard Kipling, 'The White Man's Burden', 11–12.

23. Groves and Condon, 'Teen accused of killing'. *ABC News* reports that Rittenhouse himself was part of the Public Safety Cadets, an organisation through which police forces recruit and train children and young adults 'for careers and leadership in the public safety profession'. See publicsafetycadets.org FAQ.

24. Noah Feldman, 'Kenosha Shooter's Defense Is a Gun-Rights Fantasy', *Bloomberg*, 3 September 2020; Victoria Bekiempis and Adam Gabbatt, 'Teen charged in killings of BLM protesters considered himself a militia member', *The Guardian*, 27 August 2020.

25. 'Breonna Taylor death: Gunshot at Louisville black militia protest', *BBC News*, 26 July 2020.

Towards a juridical archaeology of primitive accumulation
A reading of Foucault's *Penal Theories and Institutions*
Michele Spanò

The virtual dimensions of a project

The implicit diptych formed by the two successive courses delivered by Michel Foucault at the Collège de France between 1971 and 1973 – *Penal Theories and Institutions* and *The Punitive Society* – has already been the object of substantial commentary. The principal gains arising from philological or speculative soundings of these courses can be easily placed under two very general rubrics: first, the relation – never so explicit nor seemingly so benevolent – that Foucault entertained with categories drawn from the Marxian workshop; second, the function – never as central but no less ambiguous for that – that he assigns to law. Two rubrics that seem to flaunt a decisively anti-Foucauldian character, if the run-of-the-mill and vague understanding of his genealogical project generally connects a description of power relations irreducible to relations of production, on the one hand, with a visceral and obsessive critique of the 'juridical' form of power itself, on the other.

The following brief remarks have as their sole aim to highlight the friction between an enduring and resistant kernel of Foucault's work – the explicit and dual repudiation of economism and juridism – and this *Urtext* of his research. Yet it is these two seemingly spurious and apocryphal dossiers – the Marxian connection and the focus on the juridical – that make the conjoined and convergent reading of the two courses a reasonable proposition. These courses are not drafts or precursors of *Discipline and Punish* (published just two years after the last lecture in *The Punitive Society*), but veritable fossil remains that indicate a possible and different 'solution' to Foucauldian archaeology as such (which at this juncture Foucault chooses to call 'dynastics'). It is therefore misleading to speak of *two* dossiers. The extremely thorny question of the standing of the 'juridical' in Foucault's theoretical undertaking and the similarly slippery one of his turbulent relations with Marx's work ultimately designate a single problem: what an *archaeology of primitive accumulation* might have been and how it could have been carried out. This argument can only be formulated under a stringent condition of virtuality: while never explicitly or programmatically expressed in the pages of the two courses, it constitutes their most secret infrastructure, and Marxism and law could not but be its indispensable ingredients.

We should straightaway discount the temptation, so ambitious as to seem grotesque, of trying to verify this hypothesis. Let us immediately limit the scope of our claims and circumscribe their domain. In the following pages we will put only one of the figures of the chiasmus formed by Marxism and law under the magnifying glass, and with reference to *Penal Theories and Institutions* alone. This is but a modest probe carried out on a very restricted textual corpus.

Scene, protagonists, plot

Simply to begin to frame our discussion, it is necessary to place *Penal Theories and Institutions* in the ambit of a historiographic debate in which it ended up tacitly partaking, albeit in a Foucauldian fashion (that is to say, not frontally). I am alluding to the discussion which, between the mid-1960s and mid-1970s, interrogated the relation between the historiographic figure of the absolute state and the emergence of the bourgeoisie as a class, and which studied the effects of this relation – including popular revolts – as it prepared the take-off of modern capitalism. The elements invoked by the debate orbited around the prehistory of class struggle and its ideological authorisation, but also concerned the definition of unprecedented political objects – whether the 'economy' or even 'civil society'. Foucault's implicit contribution to the conversation addresses the various rubrics evoked by this debate from a perspective, and with a set of analytical instruments, that are capable of drastically reorganising it.

That said, Foucault shares some crucial elements with the overall framing of the debate, namely the setting in which the *pièce* unfolds – the France of the *Grand Siècle* – and the main protagonists of the plot: the absolute monarchy, the industrious bourgeoisie and a rebellious proto-proletariat. It is the linkage between setting and plot which is instead unique: it is law (penal, but not only, as we'll see). The penal question is tackled by Foucault, in keeping with one of his most characteristic theoretical moves, by avoiding the systematic scrutiny of theories and dismissing the sociology of institutions. The analysis focuses instead on the overall functioning, on the system – the host of operations, instruments and techniques that dictate the relation of forces between two poles. Popular revolts are the objects of this verification, namely as forms of deliberate refusal of that law whose political character the analysis is establishing. Foucault undertakes the meticulous reconstruction of a revolt, that of the *Nu-pieds* (1639) – a popular sedition that chooses as its polemical target the monarchical attempt to build a centralised fiscal apparatus. This motive for revolt seems capable of federating all the social classes in seventeenth-century France. The army – both agent and beneficiary of a centralised tax levy – will turn out to be the only permanent ally of the monarchy, thereby also becoming actor and object of a metamorphosis in the exercise of justice. The definition of this 'armed justice' effectively implies the establishment of a genuinely novel repressive system. The passage that Foucault tries to outline is none other than the one leading from a feudal justice to the repressive state system with the monarchy at its head. In the context of this passage the role of the bourgeoisie is crucial; it will operate on a double register, of use and abuse, masked contestation and forthright appropriation, vis-à-vis these repressive systems, finally wearing them out after having amply prejudiced them for the cause of accumulation, in the form of the Code and the protection of the capitalist freedom of exchange.

The stakes

Let us line up two substantial samples from *Penal Theories and Institutions* and listen to Foucault:

> The danger to feudalism represented by plebeian town-country contacts and an urban (people-bourgeois) coalition made a certain system of repression necessary (in the seventeenth–eighteenth century). It was only lifted during the short moment when the bourgeoisie needed this contact and political coalition to liquidate the remains of the feudal regime and its forms of tax levy. But it had to re-establish it immediately (in new, much more coherent and much more manageable forms) for it was under the shelter of this double political separation (town/country, people/bourgeoisie) that capitalism developed in the interstices of feudalism; and it still needed this double separation.[1]

And:

> The bourgeoisie under the Revolution, but especially in the Napoleonic period, carried out a separation:
> – it truly got rid of feudal (seigneurial or parliamentary) justice, which, due to its form and purpose it could not use;
> – it rejected the purpose of the new repressive system which was established in the seventeenth century (imposition of feudal rent) but not the form (or certain formal elements at least: the police element).
>
> It uses these elements for its own ends. And these ends are no longer the imposition of feudal rent, but the maintenance of capitalist profit.
>
> But whereas the monarchical regime had juxtaposed two heterogeneous repressive systems, even though both were intended to preserve feudal taxation, the bourgeoisie will give itself a unitary repressive system: State-controlled, juridical and police. A unitary system which the bourgeoisie will seek to hide beneath the assertion that justice is independent
> – of political control by the State
> – as well as the armed police force.
>
> And this is in order to get it to function as if it were an arbitral and neutral power between the social classes.[2]

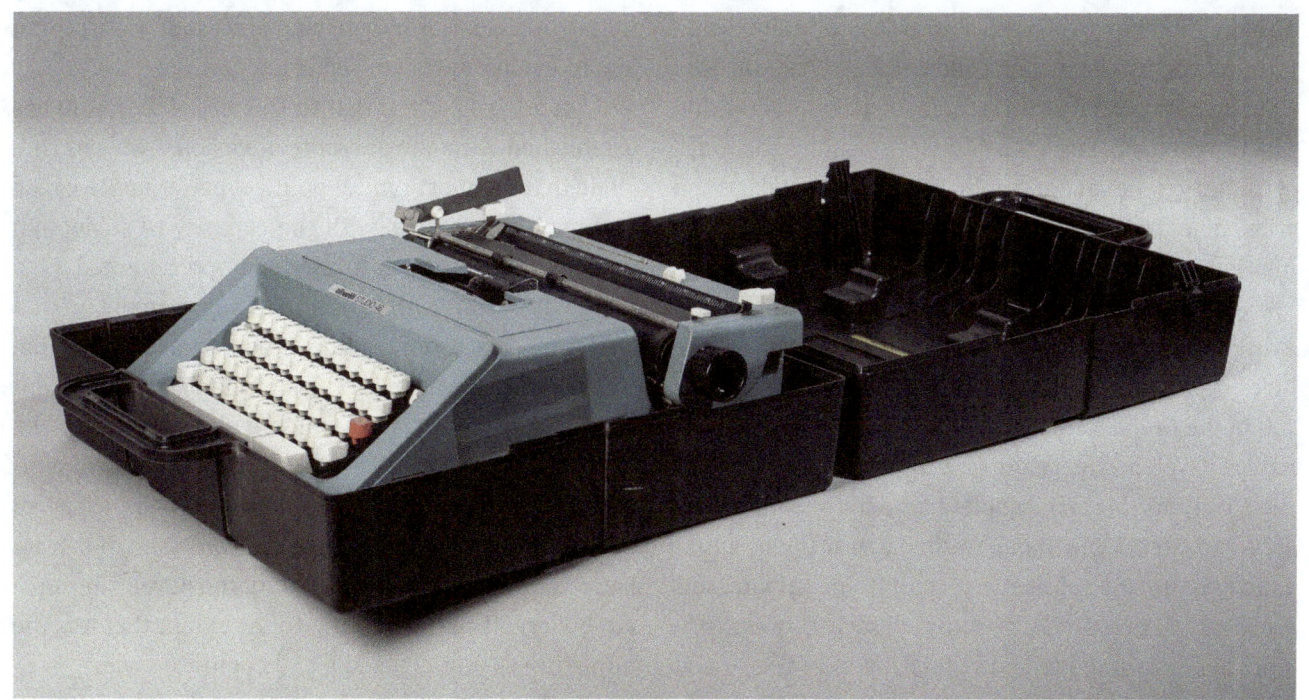

This minimal sequence sampled from Foucault's lectures condenses, in a kind of shorthand, the entire stakes of his research: to establish the role and function of (penal) law in the bourgeois organisation of a society of exchanges. But what is particularly important is that as soon as an investigation of this kind is put into motion it cannot avoid revoking the very centrality of penal law which appears to govern it. In other words, to write the history of how the bourgeoisie sabotaged absolutist penality is already to begin to narrate the vicissitudes of modern private law. What unfolds before Foucault is thus a scene that is far more crowded than he might have anticipated, and which forces him, albeit in a cursory manner, to return to the all-too-slight explanation he had initially adduced for the place that law occupies in the framework of 'dynastics'. This perpetual oscillation that traverses the groundwork of *Penal Theories and Institutions* with abiding intensity, and which finds its epicentre in law and its seeming intractability, is also the most powerful warrant for the text's posterity.

But let's not get ahead of ourselves. The semiotic square that Foucault outlines – with monarch, army, bourgeois and rebels at its apexes, and penal law and fiscal policy at its core – occludes a more viscous density. On closer inspection, it is the battlefield for a far more radical conflict between juridical regimes: the one which, by opposing them, also begins to render more solid and distinguishable the respective districts of public, criminal and private law. It is around the question of the link between patrimonial and political power – irredeemably intermingled as they are in a feudal regime – that a drastic bourgeois repair of penal law will come to operate. Stated with extreme concision, the reading hypothesis is as follows: *Penal Theories and Institutions* details the dynamic that separates two different political uses of penal law. We will call the first *tragic* or splendid, and the one that succeeds it *novelistic* or parsimonious. If 'dynastics' are, in keeping with its Foucauldian definition, a stylistics of power regimes, it is preoccupied here with the description of a crucial passage in the history of normativity, namely the use that an aggressively ambitious bourgeoisie – an economic class that is not yet a political subject – made of the penality typical of the absolutist state, in the end radically transforming its kernel after having long exploited its husk.

The story that Foucault reconstructs is therefore that of the use (or abuse) of penal law undertaken by the bourgeoisie in the fundamental shift from its marriage of convenience with absolutism to its definitive access to political protagonism and its sole management of the dialectic between public and private – the most indispensable warrant for its political existence. The penal machine devised by absolutism will thus come to be employed by the bourgeoisie in ways that transform that machine from top to bottom, along with the political and juridical conditions that had allowed it to function. This transformation completely reconfigures the standing and function of penal law. If absolutism embodies the indiscernibility of penal and public law – which finds in the crime of *lèse majesté* its most exemplary and clearest exhibition – the bourgeoisie subordinates penal to a private law which, as the veritable infrastructure of the political existence of that class, ends up turning penal law into a mere expression of its private counterpart.

In the *Grand Siècle*, two phenomena converge which, having developed in a more or less parallel manner until then, only attain their complete form in the nineteenth century. On the one hand, we find a vast process that concerns the relations between public and private, sovereignty and property, state and civil society, and which coincides with the gradual separation of property and public power; that is to say, to sum it up in a formula, with the gradual privatisation and individualisation of property. Absolutism is therefore still an episode in the history of normativity in which it is legitimate to speak of a *private property of public power*.[3] Accordingly, feudal constitutional form wholly absorbs penality as a function of political command. On the other side, there is an emergent bourgeoisie which contracts with absolutist power to be delegated the administration of public order. The monarch and the army are tasked with the sumptuous and gory repression of everything that may trouble that accumulation process which occupies a bourgeoisie that is literally 'dissociated' in its political existence as a social class demanding from an 'obsolete' political-repressive system the guarantee of its own future existence as a political class.[4] Therefore, if absolutist penality is ideologically secure it is already working towards its own abrogation: the means may well still be those of sumptuous torture but the ends are already the prosaic ones of a guarantee of social peace as the only possible background for the industrious laboriousness of the civil society of exchanges. To borrow a lapidary formula from Althusser: 'In the labour of centuries that was required to constitute and, consequently, unify the dominant bourgeois ideology, *legal ideology* [*l'idéologie juridique*] *was determinant and philosophy was dominant*.'[5] The phenomenon is therefore the same in the two cases: a public law that seems to find in penality its seal and its banner, to the point of becoming almost indistinguishable from it, begins to be shadowed by a general process of privatisation and individualisation of rights and law.

Adopting a pattern that the history of literature has established with considerable precision,[6] we can conclude that the most typical political performance of the bourgeoisie coincides with the capacity to subject an anterior juridical form to uses so unprecedented as to render it obsolete, setting up its replacement with a new form, one more suited to the task at hand. If the 'splendour of torments' is the morphological equivalent of baroque tragedy (with which it shares a space: the Court; a hero and his character: the violent prince; style: the sublimity of its verse) then discipline – in which penal law is entirely subordinated to the command of private law – is destined to play the part of the novel: the eminent bourgeois narrative form to the extent that it is the miniaturised encyclopaedia of its political style.[7]

To these two economies of power there correspond two political economies. If absolutist penality – both celebrated and consumed, exalted and sanctioned by the staging of torture – is intrinsically anti-economic, this is true not just in the more obvious sense of the wastage of energies and resources it implies, but in its logical opposition to the government of a civil society that must coincide with market exchange: a government whose juridical tools are no longer derived from penal law – which could remain the hegemonic normative register only until patrimonialism and *puissance publique* merged to the point of indiscernibility – but from private law, which will also end up governing all the residual, albeit not inessential, performances of the former. We could even affirm that the penality which is discussed especially in *Discipline and Punish* is actually only the *peripheral form* employed in the management of all those relations, or better yet all those subjects, who are incapable of adapting to the capital-relation that private law – driven by the brand-new infrastructure of subjective law – has begun to institute and with which it is delineating the institutional as well as anthropological profile of a market society. What we witness here is not a (capitalist) mode of production emancipated from a (feudal) constitutional form demanding through the dogmatics of contract a new formal government. Instead, the latter which, by instituting the social in the guise of the exchange relation also fatally undermines the confusion between patrimonialism and public power and, along

with it, the hegemony and ideological intrusiveness of penal law and repression. In other words, penal law stops being the juridical appearance of political majesty and becomes the *extrema ratio* overseeing the administration of the inevitable remainder of the private law-driven production of the bourgeois order of manufacture and exchange.

If, as Étienne Balibar has written, modernity harbours 'multiple ways of positing relation',[8] the *Grand Siècle* is the site of a fundamental epochal passage in which the relation of feudal subjection and the confusion between patrimony and the public authority that guarantees its reproduction begins – albeit in a masked and negotiated form – to be supplanted by the social relation of capital. That social relation is instead defined by a sharp separation between private property and public sovereignty, between two regimes of obligation – general law and the private contract – which are made possible and nourished by the machine of subjective right, the indispensable logical and metaphysical structure to initiate the dismantling of absolutism and manufacture a society of (waged) individuals.

This astonishing reset of juridical regimes establishes a new chapter in the history of normative rationalities. It is constituted by the shift from a primacy of the public or its fundamental merging with the penal – attested by the radical confusion between patrimonialism and public power – to an unequivocal primacy of private law, which turns penal law into a modest region which is then articulated with private law in an auxiliary and dependent manner. The dialectic between economy, politics and society is thoroughly reconfigured. A new way of formalising and disciplining the production and circulation of wealth requires a new role for penal law, which is now entirely governed by the categories of private law. This is what, commenting on the effective realisation of this process, is affirmed by way of shorthand in a phrase from *The Punitive Society*: 'The wage contract must be accompanied by a coercion that is like its validity clause.'[9]

An unintentional discovery

Not only is the story of accumulation revealed to be a juridical one through and through, but in it the starring role is not played by that penal law with which Foucault all too often identified law *tout court*, stressing the homology between penal law and the distinctive economy of sovereign power. Paradoxes of Foucault: while this insight is at the centre of *The Punitive Society*, where it attains an astonishing degree of completeness, it will be almost entirely dropped in *Discipline and Punish*, based on a framework in obvious if tacit (as the courses were intended to remain unpublished) discontinuity with the path explored up to that point.

But we need to introduce a further complication into this seemingly legible palimpsest, which also explains the break between the 1971–73 courses and the 1975 book. To put it as synthetically as possible: Foucault ends up considering the absolutist configuration of law – the one that unites and confuses the penal and the public – not as a moment in the history of normativity but as nothing less than the most proper character of law as such. It is not possible here to track the effects of this *quid pro quo* but this is certainly what prepares the ground for that image of (sovereign) power indissolubly tied to its 'juridical' character (the very ambiguity of the expression, midway between tautology and allusion, would deserve not just further investigation, but a symptomal reading). Since the adjective 'juridical' coincides for Foucault with the capacity to emit sanctions (and even with the expenditure, pomp and pleasure of doing so) then law as a whole ends up being drawn into the orbit of penality, punishment, command and repression. By deciding to treat this configuration of the relations between the political and the juridical as though it were an invariant and not a historically situated modality, Foucault blinded himself to another history of law: the history of that private law which, when all is said and done, will be the operator of the emergence of a bourgeois form of politics and a stringently capitalist organisation of the market economy.[10]

But there's more. This same blindness condemns Foucault to depicting the history of penal law in far too monolithic and inflexible a manner. Once his angle of vision has made penal law indiscernible from law *tout court*, it is much the same whether the punishment comes from an absolute monarch or a revolutionary parliament. This risks losing sight of the fact that the modes and styles of punishment, the relevance of the specificity of the offence, or the intrusions of penality into the general government of society crucially depend on the political use of penal law. If the latter does not coincide with the totality of law, then it can drastically change in standing and function in a framework in which private law (which, in an anti-absolutist guise, presents itself as neither public nor penal) is the *dispositif* capable of totalising the political field, articulating it with new and autonomous spheres (the social, the economic, or better the social understood as market). In sum, in *Penal Theories and Institutions* and *The Punitive Society*, Foucault described nothing other than the intimate connection between the emergence of the bourgeois political form (in Marxian terms, the process of primitive accumulation not so much as the historical but the *logical* premise for the institution of the modern capital-relation) and the delineation of a new dialectic between public, private and penal law (which shifts from precondition for the exercise of sovereign power to an almost peripherical articulation of the system of private autonomies). To repeat a slogan we already rehearsed above: a juridical archaeology of primitive accumulation. However, because of that very anti-juridism and anti-economism that he seemed to be dismantling in those courses, Foucault ended up blocking the way to a further development of this path whose blatant originality lies entirely in what separates it from *Discipline and Punish*. With the added paradox that in so doing he seems to retain the most vulgar part of Marxism (the reduction of law to superstructure) and to drop the most promising one (the possibility of undertaking a critique of law that would employ the same instruments that had made possible a critique of political economy).[11] It seems legitimate at this point to cease considering *Penal Theories and Institutions* as a mere sketch or draft of *Discipline and Punish* and to see it instead as the outline for an investigation that is still waiting to be undertaken.

Parallelisms

To (almost) conclude, I offer two suggestions to carry on the inquiry. First, let's change the scene and cross the Channel. The period is the same, the mid-1970s. E.P.

Thompson is working at the University of Warwick and, along with a collective formed by young colleagues and students, he organises a seminar devoted precisely to the relation between penal law and the 'prehistory' of capitalism. *Albion's Fatal Tree* constitutes the formidable proceedings of this seminar.[12] Once again, it's a question of explaining what the relation is, if there is indeed one, between (capitalist) economy and law. But, once again, and just as happened to Foucault, the path into verifying the nature of this nexus is penal law. Especially in the extraordinary opening essay by Douglas Hay – which is a kind of summation of the collection's political spirit and methodological approach – the impasse is blatant: repression and punishment seem to be the only service that law brought to bear in the aim of imposing unto a riotous and rebellious society the anthropology and politics of private property.

This argument comes with a paradoxical corollary: if, on the hand, Hay insists on the resort to penality as the royal road to the protection of an exclusive and individual right of property, one that was still exposed by dint of the legacy of feudalism to a multiplicity of regimes of appropriation, on the other, he relentlessly insists on an ideology of law that would have constituted the shared vocabulary of the bloody standard-bearers of the new property and the daring defenders of the old regime. This ubiquity of law is ultimately the fundamental discovery of Thompson and his co-authors; but if in *Albion's Fatal Tree* it struggles to emancipate itself from its standing as ideology, it is only in the sole-authored book that Thompson publishes that same year – *Whigs and Hunters* – that law crosses the threshold of autonomy and thus ceases to be solely the ideological and superstructural justification of this radical transformation in the modes of living and producing, becoming instead the most robust of infrastructures.[13] What separates two books written over the same months by the same person? The insight that penal law undergoes a radical dislocation in the period spanning the seventeenth and eighteenth centuries. If it is the ideology of property (as Hay himself demonstrates, the number of penalties carried out by comparison with the offences calling for them is singularly modest), it is only because private law is its matter.

The relationship of *Albion* to *Whigs* seems to be – albeit in inverted order – the same as the one between Foucault's two courses and *Discipline and Punish*. Thompson and his colleagues begin by overestimating the role of penal law and end up reassessing the instituent role of private law in the process of primitive accumulation. This brings with it a more general revision of the standing of law in a materialist research programme whose aim is to explain how, when and why something like the modern capital-relation could come to be instituted. Foucault seems to proceed in the diametrically opposed direction: if in the courses he appears to grasp the complex and historically sophisticated dialectic that changes the place of penal law within the process of the construction of the bourgeois form of politics, in the 1975 book that insight is submerged and discipline – whose juridical consistency is, in its status as a supplement to the contractual relationship, strictly dependent on private law – becomes the name of another (and equally formidable) project.

A different ending

A second (and final) suggestion. Allowing ourselves some license, we could propose by way of deliberate paradox and provocation that if Foucault had followed through the insights elaborated in *Penal Theories and Institutions* and *The Punitive Society* he wouldn't have written *Discipline and Punish* but rather *The Prison and the Factory*.[14] The research programme behind this work, undertaken in the same years, could be more or less superimposed onto Foucault's. It seems that here the hypotheses at the basis of Foucault's courses were coherently developed. We could therefore try to read *The Prison and the Factory* as a possible outcome of that mission statement that Foucault had left in draft form. Melossi and Pavarini's historical demonstration of the origin of the prison as 'disciplinary' before it was 'penal' illuminates an even more binding nexus between the process of accumulation and private law: the prison is not in the first instance a place of punishment and repression but a *workplace*, a space of apprenticeship into the capital-relation. The terroristic and deterrent function of the prison is thus also logically subsequent to its disciplinary one. To put it in a juridical register: there exists a contractual (private) matrix for (penal) incarceration. Penalty and obligation thus share the same logical form at their origin. This and none other would be the great bourgeois (and liberal) insight:[15] to have done with the dissipation of punishment in order to reorganise, through space, the time of life.[16] The Foucauldian formula that we presented as capable of offering a shorthand version of the speculative effort undertaken in the two courses – the one that indicates in the coupling of contract and disciplinary supplement the juridical recipe for the institution of the modern capital-relation – finds here its most lucid and exacting interpretation: in sharing their form, discipline and contract are substantially the same thing. The equation between 'contractual reason' and 'disciplinary necessity' is the formalisation of the equivalence that binds penalty and wage, discipline and contract. It is only in this way that a juridical archaeology of primitive accumulation could turn into a political genealogy of labour-power. But we must stop here, where some might argue the story should begin.

Michele Spanò is Associate Professor in Law at the École des Hautes Études en Sciences Sociales (EHESS) in Paris. His research focuses on private law history and theory. His new collection of essays, Fare il molteplice. Il diritto privato alla prova del comune *[Making the Multiple: Private Law Facing the Common], will be published in Spring 2022.*

Translated by Alberto Toscano

Notes

1. Michel Foucault, *Penal Theories and Institutions: Lectures at the Collège de France 1971-1972*, ed. Bernard E. Harcourt, trans. Graham Burchell (London: Palgrave Macmillan, 2019), 44.
2. Foucault, *Penal Theories and Institutions*, 23-4.
3. See Rafe Blaufarb, *The Great Demarcation: The French Revolution and the Invention of Modern Property* (Oxford: Oxford University Press, 2019).
4. I am following here the interpretation of the *Grand Siècle* advanced by Antonio Negri for the first time in 'Problemi di storia dello Stato moderno. Francia: 1610-1650', *Rivista critica di storia della filosofia* 2 (1967), 182-220, and later perfected in his *The Political Descartes: Reason, Ideology and the Bourgeois Project*, trans. and ed. Matteo Mandarini and Alberto Toscano (London: Verso, 2006). On the same themes, see also Alessandro Pandolfi, 'Il discorso del filantropo. Genealogia dell'egemonia borghese', *Scienza e politica* 52 (2015), 85-103, and 'La dialettica della repressione. Michel Foucault e la nascita delle istituzioni penali', *Scienza e politica* 55 (2016), 131-149.
5. Louis Althusser, *How to Be a Marxist in Philosophy*, ed. and trans. G. M. Goshgarian (London: Bloomsbury, 2017), 133. For a commentary on this formula and important insights into the place of law in Althusser and Foucault's respective research programmes, see Alberto Toscano, 'A Just People, or Just the People? Althusser, Foucault and Juridical Ideology', *Consecutio temporum* 8 (2020), 163-183.
6. Franco Moretti, 'Modern European Literature: A Geographical Sketch', *New Left Review* 206 (1994), 86-109.
7. See Franco Moretti, *The Bourgeois: Between History and Literature* (London and New York: Verso, 2013).
8. Étienne Balibar, *Filosofie del transindividuale: Spinoza, Marx, Freud* (Milan and Udine: Mimesis, 2020), 23.
9. Michel Foucault, *The Punitive Society: Lecture at the Collège de France, 1972-1973*, ed. Bernard E. Harcourt, trans. Graham Burchell (Basingstoke: Palgrave Macmillan, 2015), 149. For a brilliant reading of this passage, see Mikhail Xifaras, 'Illégalismes et droit de la société marchande, de Foucault à Marx', *Multitudes* 59 (2015), 142-151.
10. See the still unsurpassed discussion in Mario Sbriccoli, 'La storia, il diritto, la prigione. Appunti per una discussione sull'opera di Michel Foucault', in *Storia del diritto penale e della giustizia: scritti editi e inediti, 1972-2007*, vol. 2 (Milan: Giuffrè, 2009), 1077-1094.
11. See Stéphane Legrand, 'Le Marxisme oublié de Foucault', *Actuel Marx* 36 (2004), 27-43, and Pierre Macherey, *Le Sujet des normes* (Paris: Amsterdam, 2014), 149-212.
12. Douglas Hay, Peter Linebaugh, John G. Rule, E. P. Thompson, Cal Winslow, *Albion's Fatal Tree: Crime and Punishment in Eighteenth-Century England* (London: Verso, 2001 [1975]).
13. For a more sustained version of this argument, see my 'Au milieu du droit. Une glose à E. P. Thompson', in *Milieu, mi-lieu, milieux*, eds. Emanuele Clarizio, Roberto Poma and Michele Spanò (Paris: Mimésis, 2020), 157-175.
14. Dario Melossi and Massimo Pavarini, *The Prison and the Factory (40th Anniversary Edition): Origins of the Penitentiary System* (Basingstoke: Palgrave Macmillan, 2017 [1977]). But see also Alessandro Baratta, *Criminologia critica e critica del diritto penale. Introduzione alla sociologia giuridico-penale* (Milan: Meltemi, 2019 [1982]), 217-284.
15. See Pietro Costa, *Il progetto giuridico. Ricerche sulla giurisprudenza del liberalismo classico*, vol. 1 (Milan: Giuffrè, 1974), 327-78.
16. This insight finds confirmation in E. P. Thompson, 'Time, Work-Discipline, and Industrial Capitalism', *Past & Present* 38 (1967), 56-97.

Dossier: Kojève on Europe and the USSR

Kojève out of Eurasia
Trevor Wilson

Accusations of Stalinism have long followed the philosopher Alexandre Kojève. In his influential seminars on Hegel's *Phenomenology of Spirit*, held in Paris in the 1930s, Kojève had claimed that Hegel saw Napoleon as the embodiment of the universal state, as a reflection of the completed circularity of his philosophical system of knowledge at the end of history.[1] Throughout his career, Kojève would regularly draw parallels to a similar relationship between his own philosophy and Stalin, defining himself as a '*Marxiste de droite*' and viewing Stalinism as another form of the homogeneous, post-historical state.[2] Robert Marjolin, an early advocate for European integration who had recruited Kojève for work in the post-war French government, wrote in his memoirs that, in his later years, the philosopher-turned-bureaucrat would frequently describe himself as 'Stalin's conscience', yet Marjolin and his colleagues merely interpreted it as a frequent joke or provocation by Kojève, meant to *épater les bourgeois*.[3]

The claim began to be taken more seriously, however, in 1999, when Vasilii Mitrokhin, former archivist for the KGB who defected in 1991, published extensive material on various Soviet intelligence operations that had been conducted in the West. Among them was the claim of the existence of a 'white Russian' philosopher in France who served as a Soviet contact during the Cold War. According to Raymond Nart, French intelligence services had been tracking Kojève since World War II, yet the release of the Mitrokhin material has since allowed those suspicious of Kojève to 'concretise a simple intuition.'[4] In RP 184, Hager Weslati furthermore outlined the contents of an unsent letter by Kojève to Stalin, found in his archive at the Bibliothèque nationale de France, where the philosopher sought to send the Soviet leader a translated version of his Hegel seminars – collaborating evidence includes the Russo-French photographer Evgeny Reis (known in French as Eugène Rubin), who briefly shared an apartment with Kojève in Paris and alleged that Kojève sought to express *philosophically* what Stalin had achieved politically.[5]

Beyond the seemingly perpetual need to pin down Kojève as a KGB agent, tangential to these debates over Kojève's relationship to the Soviet Union has been the growing question of what role his own Russian identity played in his life and work. Born Aleksandr Kozhevnikov in Moscow in 1902, Kojève emigrated to the West in 1920, first settling in Heidelberg to study philosophy before relocating to Paris in 1926. In Heidelberg Kojève wrote his dissertation on the Russian Orthodox philosopher Vladimir Solov'ev, and although Kojève quickly developed his reputation amongst French philosophers, his earliest works, including *Atheism* (recently translated into English[6]), were written in Russian. These works were generally well received by his Russian émigré reading audience – his collected papers include congratulatory notes for his first article on Solov'ev as well as an invitation from Orthodox theologian Georges Florovsky to join the Russian Society in Paris. Among the attendees of his famous seminars on Hegel were various Russian émigrés, including beloved poet Boris Poplavsky and Raisa Tarr, an influential organiser of literary events and good friend to Véra Nabokov.[7]

While it would be possible to attribute this new interest in 'Russian' Kojève to an appeal to exoticism, flamed on by a penny press need for a new Cold War scandal and Kojève's own early interest in Eastern philosophy, it is worth noting the extent to which Russian philosophy itself has sought a return of émigré thinkers to its canon since the collapse of the Soviet Union. Russia in the 1990s witnessed a surge in the publication of philosophers writing from abroad who had previously been available only clandestinely in the Soviet Union: in her book *The End of Russian Philosophy*, Alyssa DeBlasio outlines the philosophical boom of the immediate post-Soviet period, noting that in 1993 there were more active philosophy journals in Russia than at any other point in Russo-Soviet history.[8] These new journals formally reintroduced a Russian-reading audience to thinkers who had been exiled from the Soviet Union in the early twentieth century, many (if not all!) of whom were religious philosophers who populated the émigré communities in Western Europe frequented by Kojève. To complicate matters, this re-acquaintance with non-Soviet Russian philosophy coincided with the equally new publication of Western theorists and philosophers, whose views may have been sympathetic to Marxist thought but had not been deemed suitable for print in Soviet press. Thus, figures such as Louis Althusser and Georges Bataille were first published in Russia side-by-side with Nikolai Berdiaev, Lev Shestov, and other members of the philosophical diaspora.[9] As a philosopher with allegiances to both groups, Kojève joins others like Emmanuel Levinas and Alexandre Koyré, whose combined emigration from the Russian Empire and continuing relevance to continental philosophy have made their reconstruction within the canon of Russian intellectual history an ongoing scholarly project to situate Russian thought within a larger, global network.

This return to the early Kojève and his connection with Russian thought thus reflects a need both to reframe the history of Russian philosophy after the Soviet collapse as well as to do proper justice to those Russian philosophers who worked abroad but did not adhere to the often-monolithic moniker of émigré philosophy as 'anti-Soviet'. The following two essays in this issue, which are published in *Radical Philosophy* for the first time, and which constitute some of his earliest work and were written by Kojève when he still went by Kozhevnikov, position the bourgeoning philosopher within the politically complicated milieu of Russian Paris on his own terms. The essays were published in 1929 in the Parisian journal *Eurasia* (*Evraziia*), which, as its name suggests, was an influential outlet for the Eurasianism movement in Russian diaspora.

Founded in Sofia in 1920, Eurasianism proclaimed the collapse of the 'Old World' of the West and the affirmation of the 'spiritual East' as a new global hegemon, embodied in the geo-cultural bridge of the Eurasian landmass. The Eurasianist ideology quickly spread throughout Russian émigré communities, reaching from Harbin to Western Europe, yet by 1926 Paris became the centre of the movement as well as of the Russian émigré community more broadly. *Eurasia* was founded in 1928 by Lev Karsavin, a well-known émigré philosopher and close friend to Kojève: through Karsavin, Kojève would eventually meet his partner Nina Ivanoff, who was a friend of Karsavin's daughter.[10] Karsavin had founded the journal to reflect a growing left-wing of Eurasianists who came to support the Soviet regime by reconciling belief in the unique spiritual worth of Russia (as the 'unifier' of East and West) with the unique political project of communism. *Eurasia*'s editorial approach generally supported an open line of communication between the Bolsheviks and the Russian community abroad, with its contributors regularly juxtaposing Russian religious philosophers such as Nikolai Fedorov and Solov'ev with the work of Marx and Lenin.[11]

Kojève's early essays therefore allow us to orient the philosopher within a larger rift emerging between political factions within the Russian diaspora in the 1920s, namely between those who sought to make peace with the transformational cultural politics in the Soviet Union and those who instead wished to preserve a pre-Soviet Russian intellectual life abroad, in defiance of the Bolsheviks. Left Eurasianists were not alone in trying to build a bridge with the Soviet Union: the *Smenovekhovtsy* or 'Milestone changers', a group founded in Prague in 1921 and often cited as an antecedent to National Bolshevism, likewise sought continuity with both Russian nationalist exceptionalism and the Soviet experiment, even receiving money from the Soviet government to fund their publications abroad.[12] In his most recent piece on Kojève as an alleged spy, Nart claims Kojève colluded in particular with the Union of Russian Patriots, which was yet another similar diaspora organisation with links to the French Communist Party that participated in the French Resistance during World War II.

Although it hardly seems Kojève held any nationalist sentiment toward Russia, his first article in *Eurasia*, 'Philosophy and the Communist Party' (March 1929), included in this issue of *Radical Philosophy*, agrees with the Left Eurasianists and Smenovekhovtsy in viewing the Soviet Union as a positive experiment for politics and, in particular, for philosophy. Contrary to the opinion of most of his peers in the diaspora, many of whom had been exiled precisely due to these policies, Kojève views Soviet censorship as a chance to free oneself from the bondage of the European tradition, which had stagnated after Hegel and had since reached an impasse. He therefore argues that 'one can nevertheless welcome "philosophical politics" leading to the complete prohibition of the study of philosophy' as a means of developing a revolutionary, new system of thought. This argument later finds echo in his philosophy of wisdom, a similarly revolutionary form of post-historical consciousness based in a belief in the unification of humankind in the undertaking of shared action and contrasted to philosophy as a historically embedded process – as Boris Groys describes it, rather than the desire for knowledge across history, wisdom for Kojève was a post-coital satisfaction with readily available knowledge.[13]

Kojève's positive assessment of the Soviet censorship of philosophy was not without provocation, and, in a later issue of *Eurasia*, Karsavin assured readers that Kojève's article did not 'endorse censorship and violence' but rather sought to find a positive aspect of the new Soviet policies. Karsavin further criticised directly Kojève's claim that banning European philosophy in the USSR will somehow permit a new Russian philosophy, given that the philosophers endorsed by the Soviet canon (Marx, Engels, Hegel) were of the same European origin as those they replaced. Given the political stakes of the diaspora, estranged from their cultural and political institutions, one might expect that Kojève's earliest endorsement of Soviet policies is translated through the lens of Russian national identity, calling on the diaspora to accept 'the appearance of a truly new culture and philosophy, ... because it is neither eastern nor western but Eurasian, or simply because it will be new and alive, in contrast to the already crystallized and expired cultures of West and East.' Debates within the Russian diaspora on the phenomenon of communism were often difficult to divorce from broader questions of the essence of the Russian nation, spurred on by the widespread popularity of both geopolitical conceptions of Eurasia as 'the heartland' and pivot of Great Game politics (as sketched in Halford Mackinder's famous essay from 1904), as well as Oswald Spengler's organicist conception of cultures' rise and decline in *The Decline of the West* (1923).

This geopolitical dimension of the early Kojève comes more clearly to the fore in his second article in *Eurasia*, 'Toward an Assessment of Modernity', published several months later, in September 1929, and also included in this issue of *Radical Philosophy*. There Kojève outlines the collapse of European hegemony following the First World War and a growing global opposition between the United States and the Soviet Union as propagators of capitalism and revolution, respectively. He bemoans the inability of Europe's multinationalism to unite under a single European state culture, due to the power wielded by capital and financial institutions over the 'Americanophile' continent. Forced to choose between capitalism and revolution, Kojève clearly prefers the latter, claiming that 'the victory of the second would offer [Europe] the chance to realise its unity in federal forms acceptable to each of its parts, and, alone, could return to Europe a worthy and leading place in the ranks of humanity.' A victory of capitalism would ensure Europe's enslavement to capital, whereas a victorious revolution in Europe would allow for the formation of a new and vibrant culture to replace its former stagnation – not unlike what Stalin had done for philosophy in the USSR.

These beliefs contradict Kojève's well-known later political writings, however, in which his views seem to become more moderate, both 'endorsing' the American way of life as well as efforts toward a more liberal political integration of the European continent. In a now widely cited footnote to his Hegel seminars, added in 1948, Kojève went so far as to claim that the United States, and not the USSR, had already attained the final stage of communism, 'given that practically all the members of a "classless society" can acquire for themselves everything that they like, without working any more than they feel like.'[14] In his post-war years at the French Ministry of Finance, Kojève helped to negotiate the reduction of trade tariffs between European nations in the implantation of the Marshall Plan and offered advice to Charles de Gaulle on a French foreign policy that would resist pressure from the American and Soviet superpowers. Written in 1945, Kojève's memo to de Gaulle was entitled 'The Latin Empire'. In it, Kojève argued that France should strategically construct its own empire based on the cultural traditions of the Latin world. Whereas the Germano-Anglo-Saxon world was based in Protestantism, and the Soviet sphere 'increasingly on Orthodoxy', France could unify the Mediterranean countries, including its Maghreb colonial possessions, in the pursuit of an empire driven by Catholicism.

It would be unjust to insist on philosophical or political uniformity across an individual's life, as views and people change over time, yet from his earliest writings within the Russian diaspora, one can already see Kojève searching for a philosophical system based in revolutionary thinking and the creation of the new. As his work matured, leaving behind both his Russian peers and his native tongue, the direct grounding of this system in Eurasia clearly faded, allowing Kojève instead to articulate the universal philosophical system for which he is now best known and which is devoid of any national affiliation, Russian or otherwise. Nevertheless, there is little doubt that 'revolution' meant for Kojève the Russian revolutions, and that the momentous political changes that compelled him to leave his homeland informed his own philosophy of history and his attempt to produce a post-historical system of knowledge. As for Kojève's relationship to Stalinism, his personal views on Stalin, long taken in jest by his Western peers, are best understood as a clear reflection of the complicated political orientations then operative among the exiled Russian intelligentsia, in which the success of the Soviet project meant more than merely the success of communism. Instead of second-hand guesswork, vague reports from foreign intelligence and a dismissal of his political views as ironic self-indulgence, it may instead be worth taking Kojève at his word.

Trevor Wilson is an Assistant Professor of Russian at Virginia Tech. He is currently writing a book on Alexandre Kojève and Russian philosophy.

Notes

1. Alexandre Kojève, *Introduction à la lecture de Hegel* (Paris: Gallimard, 1947), 338–9.
2. The quote comes from Dominique Auffret's biography, *Alexandre Kojève. La philosophie, l'État, et la fin de l'Histoire* (Paris: Bernard Grasset, 1990), 304.
3. Robert Marjolin, *Le travail d'une vie. Mémoires 1911-1986* (Paris: Robert Lafont, 1986), 57—8.
4. Raymond Nart, 'Alexandre Kojève dit Kojève: Un homme de l'ombre', *Commentaire*, 1.161 (2018), 224.
5. Hager Weslati, 'Kojève's Letter to Stalin', RP 184 (2014).
6. Alexandre Kojève, *Atheism*, trans. Jeff Love (New York: Columbia University Press, 2018).
7. Dimitri Tokarev, 'Les Auditeurs russes "inaperçus" (Gordin, Tarr, Poplavskij) du séminaire hégélien d'Alexandre Kojève à L'Ecole pratique des hautes études 1933-1939', *Revue des Etudes Slaves*, 88:3 (2017), 495—514.
8. Alyssa DeBlasio, *The End of Russian Philosophy* (London: Palgrave, 2014), 46-7.
9. Susan Buck-Morss describes her first-hand experience of this overlap between continental and Russian philosophy in *Dreamworld and Catastrophe: The Passing of Mass Utopia in East and West* (Cambridge, MA: The MIT Press, 2000).
10. Although Karsavin was for years a major proponent of Eurasianism, he abandoned it in his later life. Karsavin eventually left France to teach in Lithuania, where he was arrested by the Soviets and died in a labour camp in 1952. See: S. S. Khoruzhii, 'Filosofiia Karsavina v sud'bakh evropeiskoi mysli o lichnosti', *Lev Platonovich Karsavin* (Moscow: ROSSPEN, 2012), 79.
11. Antoine Arjakovsky provides a thorough overview of the Eurasianist movement, its politics and its journals in *The Way: Religious Thinkers of the Russian Emigration in Paris and their Journal, 1925-1940* (Notre Dame: Notre Dame Uni Press, 2013), 117–21.
12. The *smenovekhovtsy* took their name from *Smena vekh* ('Changing milestones', 1921), a collection of essays published by the émigré community in Prague. The title of the collection is a reference to their rejection of the positions elaborated in the influential *Vekhi* ('Milestones', 1909), an earlier collection of essays where Russian philosophers, many of whom would be exiled after the revolution, publicly divorced themselves from Marxism and instead embraced an eclectic combination of Orthodox theology and liberalism. In 'changing the milestones', the *smenovekhovtsy* sought to reorient Russian philosophy again, this time in support of the Soviet Communist Party. See A. V. Kvakin, *Mezhdu belymi i krasnymi. Russkaia intelligentsiia 1920-1930 godov v poiskakh Tretiego Puti* (Moscow: Tsentopoligraf, 2006).
13. Boris Groys, *Introduction to Antiphilosophy* (London: Verso, 2012), 158. Groys claims furthermore than this vision of post-philosophical wisdom ought to be analysed precisely through the Russian philosophical tradition, which possesses a rich history of eschatological and apophatic thought.
14. Kojève, *Introduction à la lecture de Hegel*, 510—11.

Philosophy and the Communist Party

Alexandre Kojève

It is well-known that the All-Union Communist Party (Bolsheviks) – the current ruling party in the USSR – is fighting not only on an economic and political front, but also on a cultural one: it is fighting against bourgeois culture in the name of proletarian culture.* This in particular concerns philosophy. In the view of the Party, only a materialist, Marxist philosophy can express the world view of the new ruling class and new culture, and every other philosophy is subject to destruction. It is also well known that this destruction is occurring not only or merely through ideological combat, but rather through administrative leverage: the closure of university departments, the exiling of philosophers, the banning of books, and so on.

What ought to be the non-materialist and non-Marxist philosopher's relationship to this aspect of the ruling party's politics? It would seem that the answer is given in the very question, that the relationship can be only negative. It seems to me, however, that the case here is not so simple.

Of course, there can be no doubt whatsoever that the 'philosophical politics' of the Party is having a detrimental impact on currently living Russian philosophers. It has deprived those remaining in the USSR of pupils and has severed readers forced to live beyond its borders from their home culture. Both of these undoubtedly harm philosophical work. If, however, we are somewhat inclined to scepticism toward the anti-Bolshevik pathos of a landlord whose property was expropriated, or a minister who lost his briefcase, then does it not follow that, in order to be consistent, one ought to extend this scepticism to any 'philosophical' aversion toward the events in Russia from those who have lost their role as either a real or imaginary ideological leader? After all, one would hardly claim (at least openly) that the Soviet economic order was bad only because it deprives a number of people of their property status, or that the politics of the Party are no longer suitable because several political figures are not taking part. Yet are we not on the same level when we claim that its 'philosophical politics' are certainly bad since they prevent the activity of a number of philosophers?

It seems to me, if one is assessing the authentic manifestations of a people of 150 million (currently living through an intense historical period), that this cannot be based on the interests and views of particular individuals, no matter how significant or valuable they may be. Let us apply this general principle to philosophy, as well. Everything currently taking place in the USSR is so significant and *new* that any assessment of the Party's cultural or 'philosophical' politics cannot be founded on preconceived cultural values or preformed philosophical systems. We have significantly fewer chances for error if, given the prohibition of a given philosophical system, we affirm not the falsity of that prohibition but instead the uselessness of that system for the given moment in the cultural life of a people.

If, however, one cannot judge the new ruling class' fight for a new culture from the point of view of individual philosophical figures or systems, then one can nevertheless judge it based on the idea of culture generally and philosophy as such. Yet in just such a formulation the question of the Party's 'philosophical politics' can be assessed, it seems, not entirely negatively. Here is why.

After Hegel philosophy reached a stalemate. Not that since then nothing new has been founded, or that there no longer appears any major philosophical talent. Both have occurred, of course. Toward the end of the nine-

---

* First published in *Eurasia*, no. 16 (9 March 1929), page 7, with the accompanying preliminary editorial note: '*In publishing A. Kozhevnikov's article for discussion, the editors feel it necessary on their part to note that a "positive" assessment of the politics of the All-Union Communist Party (Bolsheviks) with regards to philosophy (done in the article largely polemically) is based on a recognition by the author himself of the purely negative role of these politics in the emergence of a new Russian culture and philosophy. The following article is a thesis of sorts for discussion on the theme touched upon by the author, to which the editors of* Eurasia *intend to return in the near future.*'

teenth century Western thought effectively concluded its development: philosophy closed the circle formed by its own concepts and lost its unmediated link to reality, turning into a philosophical school of 'scholasticism' in the popular, negative sense of the term. If one takes as conclusive the major results already achieved by Western thought, then there is nothing negative to be seen about this situation. But if one thinks that philosophy, in its attempt to analyse reality, should always be based on only the unmediated given and on living material, rather than on already systematically-formulated and dead material, then the current condition of Western thought cannot be considered normal. Many thinkers admit this abnormality, including Heidegger, who in the strongest terms demands an exit from the framework of already founded systems, a refusal of already formed concepts that have lost any real sense, and who aims to once again gain the ability to see things without mediation. The path chosen by him leads through an analysis of the historical tradition: through an historical analysis of fundamental philosophical concepts he attempts to discover the forms of being expressed by them. In striving toward this goal, it seems to me that one can take another path. Alongside Western philosophy, for example, one could study Eastern (that is, Indian) philosophy, which operates on completely different concepts: comparing these two different forms of describing the world, one can attempt to penetrate into a reality completely independent from any form of description.

This is not the place to elaborate a method or produce a comparative assessment of these two means of shedding the blinders on the philosophical tradition. It is important for me now merely to note that alongside these there is another conceivable, more radical remedy: precisely the complete ignorance of the philosopher of this [Western] tradition. Though the means is perhaps radical, it is hardly applicable to the individual. A human life is seemingly too short that, starting truly from the beginning, one could create anything valuable not only for oneself but for one's contemporaries as well. Yet the situation changes completely if for a philosophising subject we mean not a concrete personality but rather an entire people. Nations are generally in no hurry, and a people deprived of a philosophical tradition has undoubtedly a better chance at developing a radically new and genuinely philosophical understanding of the world than a people living in an already ideologically formed world.

After all that has been said, it may be clear why, being a philosopher, one can nevertheless welcome 'philosophical politics' leading to the complete prohibition of the study of philosophy.

The justification of such policies, however, does not yet mean the justification of the policies of the Party. After all, not all philosophy is prohibited in the USSR: materialist-Marxist philosophy is not only permitted but propagandised by the authorities. It seems to me however that such a form of administrative interference can be justified from the point of view of philosophy. Truthfully, no matter how trivial and elementary the permission of a 'united and singular' system in a country may seem, precisely due to its singularity it is unable to interfere with the appearance of real philosophy. Those whom this system does not satisfy – and only an unsatisfied person could attempt to found something truly new – will still be unable to succumb to the temptation all too available in the philosophically 'free' West: either to shift from the 'disliked' system to another one just as ossified, or to enjoy an empty, formalist, and eclectic game with concepts that say nothing. Besides, the official philosophy of the USSR is not so elementary. One can of course not be a Marxist, yet to claim that a doctrine which finds hundreds of thousands of followers the world over is nothing but an absurdity is nevertheless to run a risk. Hegelianism, even in its Marxist avatar, is undoubtedly neither trivial nor elementary: the study of Hegel himself is moreover permitted in the USSR, and a translation of his collected works is even being prepared. True, it will be more difficult to escape from the great German philosopher than from Baron d'Holbach's *System of Nature*, which for some reason considers itself a proletarian science: almost everyone is arguably stuck on Hegel, even if they succeed in freeing themselves from Marxism through him. Those who defeat and overcome Hegel however will no longer, thanks to the Party's policies, be able find comfort in any prepared philosophy but will rather be required themselves to analyse and formalise what they see. Having behind them Marx and Hegel, they will moreover not be entirely unarmed. Exposure therefore to a 'unique and singular' system will require for them a new approach to living reality.

Thus, not only the idealised but even factual philosophical politics of the Party can be justified by a philosopher. A philosopher who in no way desires confirmations of a Marxist-Hegelian understanding of the world in perpetuity can, for the time being, make peace with the philosophical politics of the Bolsheviks. He would simply adopt Hegel's observation on the 'cunning of Reason,' which sometimes forces people not out of fear but out of conscience to work hard for the benefit of something he in no way desires.

Everything said about 'philosophical' politics is also applicable to cultural politics more broadly. The Party is fighting against bourgeois culture in the name of proletarian culture. Many find the word 'proletariat' not to their taste. This is after all only a word. The essence of the matter does not change, and the essence consists in the fact that a battle is raging with something old, already existing, in the name of something new, which has yet to be created. Anyone who will welcome the appearance of a truly new culture and philosophy – either because it will be neither Eastern nor Western, but Eurasian, or simply because it will be new and lively in contrast to the already crystallised and dead cultures of the West and East – should also accept everything that contributes to this appearance. It seems to me, for the time being of course, that the Party's policies directed against bourgeois (that is, ultimately Western) culture is really preparation for a new culture of the future.

Postscript. In conclusion, several words about foreign philosophy. Its circumstances, I think, are not nearly as hopeless as it may seem from the above. It too may prepare the construction of a new culture, or at least participate in it. This however is only under one indispensable condition: it must listen attentively to everything that is happening in Russia. If it does not want to perish, it must be – as it is now common to say – consonant with the times.

A. Kozhevnikov

After completing a PhD in Heidelberg on the Russian religious philosopher Vladimir Solov'ev, Alexandre Kojève (1902-1968) moved to Paris in 1926. He published an important early text on Atheism *in 1931 (translated into English in 2018), and gave his influential lectures on Hegel's* Phenomenology of Spirit *from 1933 to 1939 (subsequently edited and published in 1947); his later, mostly unpublished texts include* The Notion of Authority *(1942/2004) and* Outline of a Phenomenology of Right *(1943/1981).*

Translated by Trevor Wilson

Toward an assessment of modernity
Alexandre Kojève

In order to speak about the future one must first recognise the contemporary moment, as it is the contemporary moment that indicates the future.*

Previous eras were defined by their culture, that is, by an organically stable system of social relations finding within itself its own ideological justification. In our times, however, culture has ceased to be a real contemporary fact. It is completely absorbed by two different primary forces: Capitalism and Revolution.

Capitalism emerged in the era of feudalism and absolutism within European culture. Once it had fully grown, capitalism imbued this culture with itself and defined the culture as a capitalist and bourgeois one (the nineteenth century). Now, that very same culture, completely absorbed by capitalism, has itself become a part of capitalism. Revolution, the growth of which was dialectically linked to the growth of capitalism, has exited a period of transitory battles and has now gained a long-term and law-abiding nature. Capitalism, having absorbed culture, itself remains essentially uncultured. Revolution, by its very nature antithetical to the present, is unable to create culture until, having succeeded, it is no longer Revolution. Present-day Europe is in its most profound sense uncultured.

The driving forces of the present that emerged within European culture have extended beyond the borders of Europe and have become forms of world unification. Capitalism, regardless of its close link to the concept of a nation (as a market competitor), aims to unite mankind through the equal enslavement of all exploited countries by a united organisation of exploiters. Revolution, stemming from the universally shared interests of the exploited and animated by an international ideology, manifests concretely in a series of mutually linked, but nationally distinct, revolutionary movements (Eurasia, China, India, Indonesia, Mexico, and so on) that contrast the equalising unitarity of capital with the federal principle of revolution. 'Culture' in the broad sense has ceased to be a real principle of any form of unification – either internal or supranational – and is instead completely abolished by either capitalism or Revolution.

Until recently, Europe enjoyed global hegemony: its culture evolved into a global culture, and the centres for capitalism and revolution were found on its soil. Now that hegemony is lost – European culture has ceased to be an effective reality, and the United States of America has become the ruling possessor and embodiment of global capitalist unification. The leadership of revolution has passed into the hands of the Union of Soviet Socialist Republics (USSR).

The 1914-1918 war was a decisive moment for Europe's loss of its global hegemony. The war could only be concluded thanks to the financial participation of the USA, to which the centre of capitalism relocated as a result. The USA changed from a country of debtors into a general lender. During the war, nearly half of the major European governments' budgets consisted of payments from the USA. Investments of American capital were a major factor in the economic life of the strongest economies in Europe (in particular Germany). Non-European markets for European countries were significantly lost, and any attempt on Europe's part to reclaim them saw not only the USA, but also fledgling Japanese capitalism, less powerful yet even more foreign to Europe, as its competitor.

On the one hand, although European war was a powerful stimulus for revolution, Europe lost its superiority here, as well. A Revolution whose success is without precedent has overturned capitalism in an entire part of the world, Eurasia, and nationally liberated the peoples of the former Russian Empire and Mongolia, establishing a self-governing economic system nearly independent of international capital and founded on the socialist industrialisation and seizure of the entire territory of Eurasia.

---
* First published in *Eurasia*, 7 September 1929.

Revolutionary movements simultaneously developed in colonies and semi-colonies, partially and fragmentedly developed in proportion to the different levels of their economic development. In conjunction with the spontaneous industrialisation of the most powerful colonial countries (in particular India and China), the movements shook the status of Europe on the world stage.

All of these events, triggered by war, were however the logical conclusion to the preceding development of Europe, as America is nothing more than an excessive outgrowth of European expansion in the greatest period of European development (the seventeenth to nineteenth centuries), and industrialisation and revolutionary movements in colonial countries are the direct result of European capitalism.

Even the war of 1914-1918 is not a random event in European history. Europe's defining feature is a multinationalism combined with an undoubted cultural-historical unity. When European culture was still alive, this multinationalism provided the European world with a particular strength and richness, in the spirit of a characteristic, spontaneous harmony. Until recently, European wars were essentially superficial and didn't destroy the unity of the European cultural world. Yet as European culture dissolved completely into capitalism, multinationalism lost any positive meaning and became nothing more than the premise for wild capitalist competition amongst nations united only by general objects of desire. The peace of Versailles did not eliminate European multinationalism but merely increased the number of potential conflicts. First-hand memory of the past war and a preservation instinct for the moment relegate the threat of war to an unspecified moment in the future. This does not make it any less real. Militaristic energy in Europe is essentially not weakening, and the imbalance between its cultural and economic base has created a situation where Europe globally maintains only one – unenviable – superiority, that of military superiority. A future war – impossible (since the European economy is not in a condition to carry the burden alone) and at the same time inevitable (since the circumstances leading to it, the international competition of capital, remain unchanged) – threatens Europe on the one hand with definitive subjugation to American capital and on the other hand with an unprecedented explosion of revolution.

The two forces however that would benefit from European war, American capital and Soviet revolution, not only do not help to re-ignite war but are the sole concrete forces preventing its occurrence. Only a complete victory of America's advanced capitalism over the fragmented and provincial European bourgeoisie, or the victory of a proletarian revolution, can give Europe that unity and stability denied to it by its national fragmentation. The victory of the first would mean the equal enslavement of Europe and its definitive reduction to the status of a culturally and economically subordinated province. The victory of the second would offer it the chance to realise its unity in federal forms acceptable to each of its parts, and, alone, could return to Europe a worthy and leading place in the ranks of humanity. It is no coincidence that while capitalist America and the USSR both work for the prevention of inevitable war (the participation of Young and Dawes in reparations[1], the Kellogg Pact, the recent speech by the very same Dawes on the question of disarmament; on the other side, the Litvinov proposal known as the Moscow Protocol), neither participate in the League of Nations. For America, the national fragmentation proposed by the League of Nations is too clearly incompatible with the capitalist rationalisation of Europe. For the USSR, it is incompatible with the true interests of the working people of all nations. The League of Nations remains a powerless and abstract, pan-European 'grand-stander'. Its pretentions for world significance, which would leave for Europe the role of world metropolis, in fact only give non-European countries (Japan and British dominions) the possibility of applying pressure on inter-European affairs, and therefore only further underline the hopeless provincialism of Europe and the hopeless loss of its world hegemony.

Thus Europe, having dissolved its culture into capitalism, lost its primacy both in capitalism and in revolution. Its culture, having recently been worldly, has become a dependent detail of provincial capitalism.

The 'crisis' of European culture is so apparent that it now occupies, in various formulations, a common place within contemporary European consciousness. Overcoming the crisis is possible only through a moment of general social and cultural renewal. It is impossible to anticipate this overcoming, as Europe is more seized by capitalism than ever before, even as it appears merely as a provincial country dependent on capital. Elements of modernity within it are reflective and dependent (this reflection is particularly acute in Europe with regard to German 'Americanophilia'). In contrast to American capitalism, European capitalism is not industrial but rather consumer-based, and therefore is deprived of an active capitalist pathos. European culture especially falls to the level of mere consumption, losing any possibility of impact on the rest of humanity.

In line with the general crisis of European capitalism and culture, political life also is undergoing a profound crisis.

In the realm of political institutions and establishments, political life is perishing due to the lack of programs and goals. Previous political slogans and goals have lost their meaning, as the very reality on which these policies should act has changed. Entire regions have been lost to policies of autonomy and to the undifferentiated control of economic forces and financial centers. Even if after the peace of Versailles one succeeded in renouncing secret treaties and secret diplomacy (which, as we all know, did not happen), secret financial diplomacy would take the place of secret state diplomacy. The politics of states, on the one hand, is being absorbed into the international play of financial-economic forces, and on the other hand within each state political life is decomposing and decaying in a fruitless parliamentary comedy and in the petty game of ambitions and the economic interests of bourgeois politicians.

The rift between politics and culture is even more irrevocable, and this is despite the feeble attempts at proclaiming cultural politics and a state culture (*Kulturstaat*). There can be no European cultural politics because there is no European culture in any true sense. The fantasy of the leaders of Europe was exhausted in the combination of a 'state culture' with an 'economic democracy.' The idea, however, of an 'economic democracy' is a vivid example of how an unprepared consciousness is unable to see what it really is: a joint-stock company, presented as an 'economic democracy' by 'democratic' organisations, whereas it is actually one of the most clear examples of financial *autocracy*, the absolute power of financial organisations over the fragmented 'democracy' of its shareholders. 'Economic democracy' turns out to be simply a new device for fooling the petit bourgeois masses by specialists of financial capital.

The most serious attempt to overcome Europe's cultural and political crisis, without leaving the framework of multinational capitalism, was Italian fascism. Despite not a small amount of political energy invested in this attempt to revive and rationalise the old bourgeois culture, fascism can only become an extraneous element of the crisis and decay. Trying to bypass the class problem through conciliation, fascism with extraordinary persistence put forward the idea of a self-sufficient and competing nation. Thus, the only talented and lively movement born from post-war Europe to a large extent merely intensified Europe's main ulcer, its national fragmentation, and infinitely increased the already infinite danger of a new war. Fascism did not create culture, as its classless and nationalist ideology is in contradiction both with the driving forces of modernity (capitalism and revolution, both class-based and international), as well as with its own home base, the base of one of the secondary provinces of international capital. Instead of culture, fascism has merely created a masquerade. No less than 'economic democracy,' fascism – albeit in a specific 'Latin' theatrical mask – plays someone else's game, the game of dominant economic forces.

After completing a PhD in Heidelberg on the Russian religious philosopher Vladimir Solov'ev, Alexandre Kojève (1902-1968) moved to Paris in 1926. He published an important early text on Atheism *in 1931 (translated into English in 2018), and gave his influential lectures on Hegel's* Phenomenology of Spirit *from 1933 to 1939 (subsequently edited and published in 1947); his later, mostly unpublished texts include* The Notion of Authority *(1942/2004) and* Outline of a Phenomenology of Right *(1943/1981).*

Translated by Trevor Wilson

Notes

1. Charles Dawes and Owen D. Young were two American businessmen and politicians who spearheaded legislation on war reparations for Germany after WWI. [Translator's note].

Independent thinking from polity

Cedric Robinson
The Time of the Black Radical Tradition
Joshua Myers

"Cedric J. Robinson finally has found a worthy biographer in Joshua Myers. This book will remind you why we must urgently read and re-read Robinson's work. A tour de force."
Robin D. G. Kelley, author of *Freedom Dreams: The Black Radical Imagination*

PB 978-1-5095-3792-1 | September 2021 | £17.99

The Summer of Theory
History of a Rebellion, 1960–1990
Philipp Felsch

"A vivid, wry portrait of West Germany in the 1960s and '70s, when terrorists in their prison cells requested the complete works of Hegel… and when reading was a more intense experience than drugs, sex, and rock n' roll."
Lorraine Daston, Director Emerita, Max Planck Institute for the

HB 978-1-5095-3985-7 | October 2021 | £25.00

An All-Too-Human Virus
Jean-Luc Nancy

"Into the craw of the pandemic, every tomorrow seems to have slid. Nancy here attempts to breathe out. In articulating the contradictions we confront and rendering the tentativeness of our situation palpable, he scans for an opening."
Professor Joan Copjec, Brown University

PB 978-1-5095-5022-7 | November 2021 | £9.99

The First Days of Berlin
The Sound of Change
Ulrich Gutmair

"Gutmair, who was on site as a young student since 1989, describes the hustle and bustle of those days without exaggerated nostalgia, without veteran pathos, but nevertheless with a view on what was possible then – and what is lost."
Der Spiegel

PB 978-1-5095-4730-2 | November 2021 | £14.99

Go to politybooks.com to order
Find us on twitter @politybooks

The problem is proletarianisation, not capitalism
A critique of Bernard Stiegler's contributive economy
Solange Manche

In the wake of the *Gilets Jaunes* movement, the late Bernard Stiegler proclaimed, in one of his final interviews: 'what I'm interested in is to put down capitalism, for good. Or to do something else in the meanwhile.'[1] Stiegler's anti-capitalist statement signals his debt to Marx, who is frequently invoked in his writings. Indeed, in the general introduction to the first volume of his imposing three-volume work, *Technics and Time* (1994–2001; trans. 1998–2011), Stiegler grounds his philosophical project on a footnote from *Capital*, taking his cue from Marx's regret that a 'critical history of technology', which would match Darwin's 'history of Natural Technology', had yet to be written.[2] *Technics and Time* seeks to fulfil this task with a theory of technological evolution. Reflecting back on his intellectual trajectory in 2003, a few years after completing *Technics and Time*, Stiegler also acknowledged the formative role played by his membership of the French Communist Party in his youth.[3] Yet, despite the importance Stiegler himself accords Marx, the issue of how Marx informs his political and economic presuppositions has been largely overlooked and overshadowed by his debts to Derrida and Heidegger. This probably accounts for why so little critical attention has been paid to the role that capitalism actually plays in Stiegler's work.*

Of the few who have addressed Stiegler's analysis of capitalism, Ross Abbinnett gives by far the most extensive account, but largely overestimates the importance of capitalism's profit motive in Stiegler's understanding of technology. Stating that, 'the historical development of capitalism is conceived [by Stiegler] as a process that begins from the calculative rationality of the M-C-M relationship',[4] Abbinnett overlooks that, for Stiegler, it is technological innovation which, first and foremost, drives historical change, inaugurating different periods in capitalism.[5] It is Watt's encounter with the English entrepreneur Matthew Boulton that, for Stiegler, simultaneously kickstarted the industrial revolution and the Anthropocene. This is a technocentrism that ignores economic factors, such as the availability of cheap labour power that was decisive in steam power's historical victory over water.[6] Tom Bunyard is more sceptical, characterising Stiegler's politics as a form of 'technoreformism', which is marked by a complete 'disinterest in [capital's] need for quantitative profit' and a classless notion of capitalism.[7] John Hutnyk, showing that many of Stiegler's supposedly new theses on technology had already been anticipated by Marx and Engels, is equally sceptical about Stiegler's claim that 'proletarianisation' is today's universal condition, regardless of actual socio-economic inequalities.[8]

Stiegler's problematic relationship to Marx and to the critique of capitalism can be traced back to his inspiration by Marx's footnote calling for a critical history of technology. What Marx is calling for in *Capital* is a history of 'the productive organs of social man [*der produktiven Organe des Gesellschaftsmenschen*]'.[9] But the French translation that Stiegler cites centralises the question of technology to an extent the German does not. Whereas in the original it is very clear that technology operates as

---

* I would like to thank Eva von Redecker for her feedback, as well as Juan Sebastián Carbonell, Ryan Heuser and Daniel Zamora for our discussions around automation, Post-Workerism and universal basic income.

a mediator that can uncover the relations involved in the production process, the French can be read to suggest that social relations originate from technology as such.[10] However, this foregrounding of technology is not simply a matter of translation, but rather, I shall argue, an intellectual context in France informed by the reception of Italian Workerism and its attention to the so-called 'Fragment on Machines' from Marx's *Grundrisse*. In this article, I seek to further elucidate Stiegler's position vis-à-vis capitalism in relation to this context – that is, not only his sidelining of capital's profit motive, but also the economic presuppositions that underpin and motivate his proposal for a contributive economy, more specifically his belief in the threat of automation and his defence of a specific form of guaranteed income, a contributive income. My argument will be that these claims and convictions are best understood in light of Post-Workerist thought and its interpretation of the 'Fragment on Machines'.

Whereas parallels between Stiegler's work and Post-Workerism have been pointed out before, his relocating of anthropology into a technologically neutral domain, requiring a technocratic politics, has not been traced back to its Workerist roots.[11] Benoît Dillet is right to notice that Stiegler's contributive economy echoes the thought of André Gorz and Maurizio Lazzarato, but he does not place it within the context of the longer history of Workerism, and in particular, the reception of the 'Fragment on Machines'; nor does he further analyse the rationale behind Gorz's and Lazzarato's economic proposals in relation to Stiegler's. Gradually, the *Grundrisse* was pitted against *Capital* by Workerism, culminating in an isolation of the 'Fragment on Machines' that allowed for the abandonment of the question of capital accumulation. This trajectory not only led to a disconnection between living knowledge and capital, as Matteo Pasquinelli argues, but equally to a teleological understanding of technological development, which I claim explains Stiegler's support for economically unjustifiable predictions about the dangers of automation.[12] This does not simply help us to understand the political implications of Stiegler's work as such but also sheds light on the philosophical rationale behind contemporary automation discourse and post-capitalist visions that have recently received much critical attention, albeit primarily in terms of their economic presuppositions.[13]

The objective of Stiegler's contributive economy is to offer a solution to the perceived economic threat of robotisation, but its primary aim is to fight the negative consequences Stiegler considers automation to have on individuation, which he also refers to as proletarianisation. As proletarianisation is primarily a problem of reason and knowledge, what a contributive economy seeks to establish is a new valuation system that rewards activities that contribute to society's general knowledge.[14] After introducing the notion of proletarianisation in relation to Stiegler's conceptualisation of technology as pharmacological, I will offer in what follows a brief overview of the history of the *Grundrisse*'s Franco-Italian reception that will serve to contextualise my analysis of Stiegler's engagement with post-Workerist thought, which is primarily mediated through the work of Gorz and Moulier-Boutang, although connections to McKenzie Wark, Antonella Corsani and Maurizio Lazzarato will also be addressed.

Proletarianisation and *pharmakon*

Proletarianisation is a concept that captures a noetic process, denoting a generalised loss of knowledge of the subject, our gradual becoming stupid. Stiegler uses the notion for the first time in the third volume of *Technics and Time* (2001), drawing upon Gilbert Simondon's reading of Marx in *On the Mode of Existence of Technical Objects*. In the first volume of *Symbolic Misery* (2004), he starts to develop the concept more rigorously, resulting in a tripartite division of proletarianisation into the loss of *savoir-faire*, *savoir-vivre* and *savoir-théoriser*, which informs his later works, such as *The Re-Enchantment of the World* (2006) and *Taking Care of Youth and the Generations* (2008). In a Heideggerian vein, *savoir-faire* denotes more practical knowledge; *savoir-vivre* corresponds to a certain know-how of living together, which he primarily explores in psychoanalytic terms; *savoir-théoriser* is quite literally a capacity for theoretical thinking. The loss of these three forms of *savoir* rests upon a historical distinction between three different economic eras, namely, that of nineteenth-century industrial capitalism, twentieth-century Fordist consumerism and our current economic paradigm.[15] This does not mean that each loss of *savoir* is mutually exclusive, corresponding to a specific and unique economic epoch. They are in fact

cumulative, and Stiegler argues that we are witnessing the loss of all three forms of knowledge today.

In this periodisation of capitalism, whereas labour in the nineteenth century is primarily considered to be characterised by the loss of artisanal skills, labour in the twenty-first century is seen to cause a loss of cognitive capacities. Stiegler holds that this damage does not only affect workers but everyone, as big data and the crowd sourcing economy replace the producer by the consumer. In 1993, with the introduction to the public of the World Wide Web, our milieu was transformed into a digital one, a milieu of absolute automation, the automation not simply of practical knowledge but also of decision-making. We are now all becoming part of the machine, as artificial organs causing 'a complete cerebral desertification'.[16] No one escapes proletarianisation in the digital age, not even the likes of Alan Greenspan, the former Chair of the U.S. Federal Reserve, who would have been made redundant by finance algorithms. Stiegler therefore speaks of an age of generalised proletarianisation characterised by the automation of everyone's knowledge, resulting from the material automation of both physical and cognitive tasks.

So, what exactly is the relation between *proletarianisation*, knowledge and automation? Stiegler can draw a direct connection between knowledge and automation because he understands noetic processes as a psycho-somatic shaping of the self that is dependent upon retentional technological conditions. Stiegler derives this conceptualisation of technology from Plato's dialogue on writing in the *Phaedrus*, specifically as interpreted by Derrida in *Dissemination* (1972). Rereading Plato's text, which Friedrich Schleiermacher had accused of merely being a condemnation of the written word as sophistry, Derrida picks up on the polysemy of *pharmakeia*, denoting the 'administration of the *pharmakon*, the drug: the medicine and/or poison'.[17] Emphasising writing's need for a material base, Stiegler considers concrete supports of memory as that which constitutes technology, which, like Plato's *pharmakon*, can be both medicine or poison.

This interdependency of memory and its own externalisation into an object or, as Stiegler argues, technological objects, leads him to define technology as *hypomnēmata* or mnemotechnics.[18] For Stiegler, technology is a very broad notion ranging from flint tools to smartphones: any material object that serves as a memory support. But Stiegler does not think of technology as merely instrumental or 'enframing', following Heidegger, but as fundamentally co-constitutive of the human, its temporal relation to the world.[19]

Stiegler distinguishes between three forms of memory, conceived in temporal terms, which he calls retentions, further developing the distinction Edmund Husserl makes between primary and secondary retentions, adding a third category of tertiary retentions. 'Primary retention is what constitutes the temporal fabric of all perception insofar as it lasts: insofar as, retaining in itself its own duration, it thus enriches its perceptual content.'[20] Consciousness has no control over primary retentions. They are purely accidental and happen to the subject. Secondary retentions are the recollections in the mind of those first retentions, which in turn are shaped by further primary retentions. Stiegler explains this back and forth process using Husserl's example of melody. When I listen to the same melody a second time, I will hear it differently from the first time since my ear has been affected by my initial experience: consciousness has altered between the two hearings.[21] In this way, secondary retentions are recollections of past lived experience, which can be spatialised, according to Husserl, in what he calls 'image-consciousness', such as art, sculptures or any other form of the expression of recollections: devices Stiegler qualifies as technological objects.

However, Stiegler identifies a problem in Husserlian phenomenology's exclusive focus on lived experience, namely, that it forgets the question of the historicity of objects.[22] From a Heideggerian perspective it would overlook a historical conception of temporality, as the already-there is always already inherited.[23] Hence, Stiegler uses the term tertiary retentions to denote those mnemotechnics in which knowledge is accumulated, not only in an individual's lifespan but intergenerationally.[24] According to Stiegler, it is this cyclical movement of the exteriorisation and internalisation of knowledge, a self-reflective dynamics that simultaneously unfolds over the timespan of an individual's life, as well as transgenerationally, that constituted reason in opposition to the rationality and calculability he criticises as characteristics of modernity. Because of the historical and collective dimension of memory retention the 'I' is always a 'we' temporally and spatially. The conceptually close notions of proletarianisation, disindividuation and denoetisation, and the automation of reason, all capture the short-circuiting of this cyclical noetic process.

In the third volume of *Technics and Time*, Stiegler draws a link between Marx's understanding of technology and his own conceptualisation of the movement of memory and knowledge, a reading that primarily draws on Gilbert Simondon's interpretation of alienation in *On the Existence of Technical Objects* (1958).[25] Marx, in the *Grundrisse*, and more specifically in the 'Fragment on Machines', describes machines as an externalisation of knowledge, or in Stieglerian terms a mnemotechnic or a *tertiary* retention, which deprives the worker of their skills or knowledge.[26] This total loss of knowledge is what, for Stiegler, turns workers into the proletariat. What Marxists fail to see is that 'the proletariat is not the working class, but the non-working class [la classe des désoeuvrés], that is, the downgraded, the class of those who are declassified. They are those who no longer know, but serve, systems that exteriorize knowledge'.[27] Following Simondon, Stiegler considers alienation to be the effect of a rupture of the fundamental continuity between the human and technology. Although he already states in the third volume of *Technics and Time*, again building on Simondon, that 'this process of worker enslavement leads to the worker's loss of individuation and displacement into the machine',[28] the cyclical nature of proletarianisation is best captured in *Automatic Society* (2015), where Stiegler describes it as 'an exteriorization without return, that is, without interiorization in return'.[29]

More concretely, the human knowledge of how something is produced is exteriorised in a machine. As a result, the worker operating the machine no longer practices the initial skills that were needed to produce whatever products the factory at that moment produces: literal automation. No longer having to learn how to master a certain skill, the worker remains skill-less, without *savoir-faire*, and becomes dependent upon technological instruments. Technical automation thus provokes the automation of knowledge, dissolving its self-reflective process. What distinguishes workers from proletarians, according to Stiegler, is that the latter are subjected to the disruption of the cyclical movement of the noetic process, the short-circuiting of memory. Harking back to the critique of modernity and its suspicion of calculability, proletarianisation explains the reification and fragmentation of reason as resulting from a disruption in memory retention that would otherwise require long-term, qualitative and reflective engagements.

The Franco-Italian reception of the 'Fragment on Machines'

Written between 1857 and 1858, the *Grundrisse* is generally considered to be the draft that lays the foundation for *Capital*. Although two sections had been published by Karl Kautsky in the early 1900s, the *Grundrisse*'s influential status in twentieth-century debates on technology took off much later due to its obstructed publication and circulation history.[30] Most importantly, for my concerns here, one section of the *Grundrisse*, the 'Fragment on Machines', became the centrepiece of post-war Italian Workerist theory: an anti-trade union and spontaneist current. Its emergence coincided with the publication of the journal *Quaderni Rossi* in June 1961, but should be understood against the larger backdrop of changes in capitalist production and social revolt.[31] The Italian focus was militant and served as a strategic fulcrum for wildcat strikes and sabotage.[32] Exploring the effects of mechanisation, Marx's distinctive arguments in the 'Fragment on Machines' resonated with the struggles that Italian workers were facing following post-war changes in manufacture.

After the Second World War, Italy saw an exodus of people from the agricultural South to the industrial North. This fundamentally changed the composition of the working class, from a body of skilled workers into unskilled workers. Workerism's proponents came up with a set of new concepts in an attempt to grasp this new working class. The 'craft worker', possessing more artisanal skills, was replaced by the unskilled 'mass worker' as the new revolutionary subject. The 'mass worker' was constituted by the assembly lines of the Fordist mode of production, which made everyone replaceable. But the assembly line also meant that small strikes were more effective. Seemingly out of touch with these developments, the trade unions persisted in their attachment to professionalism and continued to pursue their traditional bargaining techniques using the workers' skills as leverage to get capital to meet their demands. Workerists saw the mass worker as a force that could be mobilised against both capital and unions.

In 1964, Renato Solmi published the first translation of the 'Fragment on Machines' in the fourth issue of *Quaderni Rossi*.[33] Its subsequent reception history came to reflect Workerism's attempts to rethink the relations between changing class composition and technological developments driven by, and constitutive of, capital's ongoing mutations. Whereas early Workerism still read the text in the light of *Capital* – in particular the fourth section of the first volume and the previously unpublished chapter on the 'Results of the Immediate Process of Production' – it later inspired a consideration of technology increasingly independent from capital accumulation, which became characteristic of Post-Workerist thought and its diagnosis of the 'social worker'. Although in the text itself Marx foresees that science and technology will become increasingly determined by the need for capital accumulation, the replacement of the mass worker by the social worker in the 1970s prepared the way for a reading of Marx's text that only kept its teleological narrative afloat.[34] In the wake of the 1974 recession, Antonio Negri argued, for example, that, because of the tendential rate of profit to fall, capital would be pushed to the massification of abstract and intellectual labour, thereby absorbing the whole of society into the proletariat.[35] Even before Negri, Franco 'Bifo' Berardi and Romano Alquati had already written about a new class characterised by intellectual and technical labour. Negri considered the social worker to be the incarnation of a new revolutionary subject, and he saw its struggle anticipated by 'The Fragment on Machines', namely, the overcoming of the labour theory of value as a consequence of technological innovation. Building upon the notion of the 'general intellect', Negri expected capitalism's new class composition to give rise to 'a human individuality capable of communism [which would] conclude that social, proletarian, reappropriation is ... necessary'.[36] The technology question had thus always been central to Workerism's understanding of class relations, but gradually started to gain more ground as the new locus of struggle from the 1970s.

After the fall of the Berlin Wall, the 'Fragment on Machines' acquired a renewed impetus in which the antagonism to capital was no longer required. Instead, transformations in the production process, said to mark a transition from a Fordist to a post-Fordist model, were welcomed as potentially revolutionary. In 1996, Maurizio Lazzarato coined the term 'immaterial labour': a form of labour that demands workers develop new skills in relation to the emergence of new technologies and that mobilises them as subjects.[37] Instead of condemning the ways in which this new form of employability blurs the boundaries between work and non-work, Lazzarato welcomes it as a '"silent revolution" taking place within the anthropological realities of work and ... the reconfiguration of its meanings'.[38] Immaterial labour is seen as opening up space for creativity and the development of workers' autonomy, beyond the distinction between work and non-work, and mental and manual labour. Traditionally reserved for the middle and upper classes, this new potential for workers to express their creativity would thus contribute to the troubling of class relations.

It is these mutations of labour that Negri and Michael Hardt in their co-authored works consider to be a transformative force of capitalism from within, resisting commodification. Whereas in the late 1970s, Negri still held that immaterial or cognitive forms of labour could potentially function as a vector for class consciousness, in *Empire* (2001), written with Hardt, he views them as holding creative and cooperative potentials in and of themselves, planting a seed for a 'spontaneous and elementary communism', and hence abandoning an antagonistic stance vis-à-vis capital.[39] The novel infrastructures of the information economy that make workers cooperate, irrespective of their geographical location, would give rise to creativity and common action beyond measure, thus spelling out the antithesis of capitalist calculability and subverting the notion of property. Acquiring novel skills, 'the productive subject ... brings with itself, at the level of the General Intellect, an extraordinary energy that is able to break the capitalist relation.'[40] Workers would thus be able to become producers independently from capital relations. As Isabelle Garo shows, this eliminates the formal and legal dimension of ownership, reducing property to appropriation.[41]

Stiegler does not draw directly on Negri and Hardt's work, but he does on Yann Moulier-Boutang's, in particular his idea of the 'pollen economy', a notion that is conceptually very close to Hardt and Negri's thought. This proximity is not coincidental. Moulier-Boutang has worked in close cooperation with Negri since the early 1970s. Moulier-Boutang was the first to introduce Workerism into France, founding the group Matériaux pour l'invention (Materials for Invention) which translated texts by Negri, Mario Tronti and Oreste Scalzone.[42] Like Hardt and Negri, Moulier-Boutang is convinced that capital's growing dependence on cognitive forms of labour will lead to the emergence of communistic relations from within capitalism itself. He maintains that cognitive capitalism does not simply change the way commodities get produced, but unsettles the very substance and shape of value itself.[43] Extracting surplus value from knowledge and skills obtained outside the walls of the company, cognitive capitalism captures an extra-economic activity – an activity he compares to bees pollinating. What generates value in cognitive capitalism is not the honey, but the pollination process. This is a theory Gorz equally embraces.

Hacker euphoria and deproletarianisation

Within this line of thought, a great admiration for hackers and the free software movement emerged, an admiration that Stiegler shares with Moulier-Boutang, Gorz and McKenzie Wark. In *A Hacker Manifesto* (2004), Wark writes that the hacker, whom she considers constitutive of a new hacker class, produces new abstractions out of raw data. In order for the 'vectoralist class' – those who 'control the vectors along which information is abstracted' – to lay claim over intellectual property rights, the hacker always needs to produce a 'qualitatively new creation'.[44] Gorz, who adopts Moulier-Boutang's notion of cognitive capitalism, welcomes capital's new extraction model, as it means that the survival of enterprise increasingly relies upon self-organisation, creativity and the ability of people to cooperate and to excel in networks. According to Gorz, this leads to the emergence of 'positive externalities', namely, 'a collective outcome that transcends the sum of individual contributions'.[45] These positive externalities transcend quantifiability, making the subordination of human activity to the market impossible, and thereby giving rise to a new space for the full development of human capacities, to *Bildung* or the cultivation of minds. It is in free software activists and hackers that

Gorz sees potential agents for the 'transcendence of capitalism'. Gorz insists that these agents present a form of actually existing anarcho-communism, which does not seek to take power but instead demonstrates that a different world is already possible: 'There will be no revolution through the overthrow of the system by external forces. The negation of the system spreads within the system itself by the alternative practices, to which it gives rise.'[46] We are thus back at the Post-Workerist trope of the hope of change from within capitalism itself, making antagonistic politics essentially redundant.

Bearing in mind Stiegler's notion of deproletarianisation as the de-automation of knowledge, it is not a surprise that he draws on the work of Post-Workerists and thinkers inspired by this tradition, such as Gorz, Moulier-Boutang and Wark. It is exactly in their analysis of post-Fordist capitalism giving rise to a pollinating residue that Stiegler sees a new horizon of possibilities for deproletarianisation. According to Stiegler, Moulier-Boutang shows that cognitive capital positively reconfigures reason, because increased computation now makes it possible to distinguish between that which is and that which is not codifiable.[47] He considers these new technologies to enable activities that hold interpretative and deproletarianising capacities. As such, Stiegler's contributive economy seeks to implement a reconfiguration of capitalism's underlying conception of value and the remuneration model upon which it is based. Following the classic Post-Workerist understanding of capitalism's mutations, Stiegler maintains that the labour theory of value is no longer valid since value is no longer related to actual productive activities that can be measured in labour time. Instead, he maintains that wealth under post-Fordism is generated by the human activity that precedes the production of commodities, the equivalent of Moulier-Boutang's pollen, Gorz's positive externalities and Wark's notion of abstraction.

In order to describe this shift in the form of value, Stiegler rethinks the notion of work by making a distinction between work (*le travail*) and employment (*l'emploi*). He considers work to be 'that by which we cultivate knowledge'. Employment, or the hegemonic form of salaried work under capitalism, destroys this work. Employment is a proletarianising activity, whereas work is its antidote.

> Employees do not work, in the sense that working, which means to individuate oneself, which means to invent, to create, to think, to transform the world. Work is that which we used to call oeuvre [*l'ouvrage*]. In the word 'oeuvre' [*ouvrage*], you can hear the verb 'to open' [*ouvrir*], 'to work' [*ouvrer*] meaning to operate. A worker opens a world that can be a very small world but nonetheless a world.[48]

Work is thus that which enables the subject to individuate themselves, to become singular. In Stiegler's thought, the subject shapes itself in relation to its environment, a process that is always thought as psychosomatic. Ultimately, this means that the potential of a subject can only unfold when they are engaging with their milieu and shaping it, as much as it shapes them. Although not directly referring to Gorz when making the distinction between work and employment, Stiegler cites him when defining true work as a *poiesis* that answers an individual's need, in Gorz's words, 'to appropriate the surrounding world, to impress his or her stamp upon it and, by the objective transformations he or she effects upon it, to acquire a sense of him- or herself as an autonomous subject possessing practical freedom'.[49]

The teleology of technology

The hope of the Post-Workerist tradition that technological development would bring forth communist relations from within capitalism has been criticised for its teleological vision of technology. Frederick Harry Pitts, for example, notes how Hardt and Negri's imaginary of the overcoming of capitalism is driven by 'a teleology … which suggests that social actors rise to prominence because of the forces of production and can only reshape the relations in so far as the forces permit.'[50] Whereas Pitts places an emphasis on the deterministic tendencies of their vision, Riccardo Bellofiore and Massimiliano Tomba recognise how Hardt and Negri uphold a linear scheme anticipating 'the quantitative extension of so-called immaterial labour', which they argue is not supported by any actually existing economic tendencies. The problem with this account for Tomba and Bellofiore is that it 'is blind to how different forms of surplus-value extraction intersect with one another'.[51] Even if it is true that technological innovation does not automatically translate into a universal and homogenous profit model or a global standardisation of forms of labour, the assumption that underlies this reductive view of the world economy is its isolated understanding of technological development, disconnected from larger political questions and macroeconomic dynamics.

To some extent, Stiegler nuances this optimistic teleology by adding his notion of the *pharmakon* to the equation. Indeed, Stiegler criticises the Post-Workerist tradition and concepts such as cognitive capitalism and immaterial labour for their idealism, that is, their failure to take into account the materiality of new technologies, seeing them as a neutral mediation allowing for the expansion of mental and affective work.[52] Directly opposing Gorz, Stiegler criticises the notion of the immaterial, stressing that the type of employment that these technologies allow still requires the actual existence of material devices. According to Stiegler, we should thus not consider capitalism's industrial phase as a story of the past, since an information driven economy in fact requires the mass production of material supports. He uses the term 'hypermaterial' to denote that matter and form are no longer distinguishable in today's energy and information complex. Within this logic, information would present itself as a form but is inseparable from its material base, the technological object that allows for its dissemination. Since technology is the support of memory, of its externalisation, but equally that which allows it to unfold, it is irrelevant to separate matter from the supposedly intangible faculty of knowledge. Hence, taking into account how a material object can both trigger the curative and toxic dimensions of itself, Stiegler avoids falling into the trap of predicting a future that will necessarily be devoid of alienated labour.

There is however another teleology of technics central to the thought of Gorz and Moulier-Boutang that Stiegler does not question, and which forms one of the pillars of his contributive economy: the inevitability of unemployment caused by automation.[53] Both Gorz and Moulier-Boutang consider technological innovation to be the cause of job destruction. Moulier-Boutang even predicts an unprecedented catastrophic wave of unemployment caused by the automation of mental tasks.[54] To support this, Stiegler refers to the commonly cited 2013 study by Carl Frey and Michael Osborne, in which it is claimed that 47% of US jobs are susceptible to being automated within the next decade or two.[55] As Aaron Benanav and Kim Moody show, however, even if labour conditions are worsening, automation can hardly be held responsible for it.[56] In fact, rather counter-intuitively, technological innovation and automation typically bring about a boost of employment, as prices fall in relation to productivity.[57] This was also the case in the automobile industry. In 1961, when General Motors introduced the first robot, the unimate, employment grew in that sector. The same holds true for logistics and warehousing today. The countries that have the highest levels of robotisation equally have the highest trade surplus, helping to maintain jobs rather than destroying them. Of course, this does not mean that the phenomenon of technological unemployment is entirely non-existent, but it is complex, involving periods of economic crisis, low investment in technology, deepening stagnation and financialisation.

When looking at the specific case of France, which is nonetheless representative of a general tendency in high-income countries, unemployment drastically rose in the 1970s. This fall in employment was primarily the effect of globalisation and competition, itself part and parcel of cold war history. Wanting to prevent the spread of communism, the US decided to share its technological advantage with its competitors Japan and Germany. Devaluating their currencies, European and Japanese products became more competitive, which in turn put pressure on the US. It became a race to the bottom, competing for market shares, leading to an overall plummeting of growth and thus also a drop in investments in new technologies at the expense of long-term investment in fixed capital.[58]

Even if, historically, there is no evidence that automation is the absolute cause of mass unemployment, this does not necessarily mean that it could not happen in the future, but there are few indications that this will in fact be the case. For the moment, technologies that are often cited as having the potential to put people out of work *en masse*, such as self-driving vehicles and trucks, are very unlikely to see the light of day during our lifetimes.[59] Even on a purely technological level, as Jason Smith also observes, robots are still very far from performing simple tasks.[60] The economic problem behind this is perhaps not the inherent complexity of certain tasks, but rather investment. Given the current global market's unpredictability, firms tend to favour short-term investments. This leads to capital expenditure on already existing technologies. A survey led by the World Economic Forum even shows that senior executives themselves do not think technological innovation will bring most changes to working conditions and employment. Rather they expect above all short-term profitability, pressure by shareholders and new management methods to alter the future of work.

As Pasquinelli points out, Workerism's gradual isolation of the 'Fragment on Machines' from the rest of Marx's oeuvre made it possible to separate the question of living knowledge from capital. He shows that Marx drew deeply on Charles Babbage's project to mechanise mental labour, a project underpinned by what Pasquinelli refers to as Babbage's labour theory of the machine, which states that 'a new machine comes to imitate and replace a previous division of labour.'[61] Whereas Marx follows Babbage in his analysis of the division of labour of physical tasks, the history of Artificial Intelligence underwent the same process, derived from the division of labour in mathematics.[62]

If the history of mechanisation is the history of the standardisation of tasks, including mental tasks, this problematises Stiegler's hopes for new technologies being able to de-automate knowledge. Wark, looking back on *A Hacker Manifesto*, recalls that the millennial dream of escaping commodification was perhaps too romantic a view.[63] The information economy has led to anything but the weakening of reification. The real problem in the history of the reception of the 'Fragment on Machines' is perhaps not the separation of the question of living knowledge from that of capital, but rather the more general isolation of the question of technology from capital accumulation. As Stiegler's work demonstrates, the afterlife of the text made it possible to analyse the materiality of knowledge completely independently from the problem of profitability, which is more complex than productivity rates, especially in a globalised and financialised economy.

Contributive income

Nonetheless, Stiegler's philosophy should not simply be dismissed on the basis of an inaccurate understanding of the global economy. It is also a response to the deteriorating state of capitalism today, which revealed itself with the 2007-8 financial crisis, and to the restraints that today's politico-economic status quo impose on our lives. Although Gorz, Moulier-Boutang and Stiegler justify the urgency of a form of guaranteed basic income because of automation's immanent threat, Stiegler's main concern is the degrading conditions of possibility for the unfolding of people's lives. Basic income is politically conflicted. Once promoted by Milton Friedman, it is currently defended by Silicon Valley gurus Elon Musk and Zuckerberg, as opposed to the more progressive proposals on the Left that typically stress its potential to liberate time from the logic of the market.[64] In the Post-Workerist tradition, basic income is a response to the condition of immaterial labour and Moulier-Boutang's pollen economy, but it has roots in the earlier Workerist concept of the 'social factory', coined by Mario Tronti, according to which value extraction under post-Fordism largely takes place outside of the factory's walls.[65]

Stiegler's model for a basic income is most directly indebted to Gorz's proposals for a 'second cheque' and Corsani and Lazzarato's study of the French social support system for workers in the arts and entertainment industry, *L'intermittence du spectacle*.[66] Gorz imagines a two-part redistributive system that seeks to reduce labour time, creating free time for human flourishing. Renumeration would be based on the contribution to society's general productivity and would be complemented with a second cheque.[67] With the advent of the internet and the expansion of immaterial labour, Gorz however came to support an unconditional form of basic income, on the basis that technological development would decrease the need for productive labour.[68]

Whereas Gorz insists that a guaranteed form of income needs to be absolutely unconditional to avoid the risk of the commodification of tasks once you link remuneration to an obligation, Stiegler is concerned that liberated time will be captured by the market turning it into a time of consumption, which again proletarianises the consumer.[69] He therefore turns to Corsani and Lazzarato's research on entertainment workers to supplement his blueprint for a contributive income, the aim of which is to gradually expand the intermittence redistribution system to the whole of society.[70] Stiegler's contributive income is a conditional form of income that remunerates the transmission and acquisition of knowledge and know-how. It rewards deproletarianising activities or general knowledge contribution to society. Like Gorz's second cheque and *L'intermittence du spectacle*, contributive income complements other sources of income, such as temporary forms of salaried labour.[71] What Stiegler finds appealing in this system is that it rewards non-commodified activities that are valuable to society as whole, in their deproletarianising potential.

> In principle, this conditionality of contributive income does not bother me. Because it is this income that would allow the system to become solvent, by encouraging the free sharing and valorisation of knowledge in all layers of society and for all types of jobs, in the way it is happening in free software.[72]

Oddly, since a cap is never mentioned, the objective is to incite people to devote ever more time to work rather than to employment, whether this is considered in economic or non-economic terms. Like the intermittence model, Stiegler's contributive economy envisages a highly flexible individual, who could never have a clear indication of their monthly income, as it varies according to what extent they manage to combine a set of varied tasks, which are not excluded from the corporate sector. Besides the fact that it does not fundamentally question capitalism itself and opens up a way of working with corporate business, it offers no guarantee against self-exploitation.

The implementation of the contributive income would seek to remunerate 'individuals in terms of the development of their knowledge and capacities outside of working hours and on the condition that they valorise periods of intermission within the contributive economy's activities'.[73] Instead of advocating a right to laziness, Stiegler conceives of the deproletarianisation of knowledge not only as a right but also as a duty.[74] How this legal aspect of this duty would concretely be realised is unclear, but he envisages it as constitutive of a new order of law that should not be enforced using its habitual institutional framework. This raises the question of who will lose out in this new social valuation system. What happens to those people who are not able to become the agile and self-innovating individuals that Stiegler envisages? He acknowledges that not everyone can contribute to society in this way – people to whom he somewhat degradingly refers to as 'fragile characters' – which is the reason why he equally supports an initial minimum and unconditional subsistence income.[75]

Realising a contributive economy

Stiegler's proposal for a contributive economy has been experimented with in a conglomeration of three communes (Saint-Ouen, Saint-Denis and Aubervilliers) of the Metropolis of Greater Paris: Plaine Commune, also referred to as a 'contributive learning territory', primarily financed by the general budget for Greater Paris. Counting nearly half a million inhabitants, they are also the most precarious of the Île-de-France region.[76] Building upon pre-existing infrastructures, the first steps taken by Plaine Commune are to improve the employability of its inhabitants, educating them for a changing labour market that increasingly demands digital skills. Plaine Commune works with the research group Ars Industrialis (AI) and L'Institut de Recherche et de l'Innovation (IRI), which was formally directed by Stiegler, and the project directly draws on Stiegler's thought, referring to his concepts of proletarianisation and transindividuation throughout.[77] Collaborating with the companies Orange and Dassault Systèmes, the aim is to build new online platforms that seek to deproletarianise its inhabitants. Involving researchers, AI and IRI try to bend public education into a professionalising orientation, adapting to the corporate demands related to technological innovation and smart city urban transformation. Unsurprisingly, Orange and Dassault help to finance these research positions because they get guaranteed market shares in return. The general scheme appears to be that of making the region attractive for investors and employers, which corresponds to Stiegler's conviction that profit is absolutely necessary for investment. Mirroring the overall Post-Workerist faith in working from within capitalism itself, this blending of the private with the public sector is more reminiscent of a neoliberal rationale than it is of the Marxian notions it nonetheless mobilises.

The importance of tracing Stiegler's economic presuppositions is thus not only to understand his thought better but to interrogate its wider political implications and shortcomings. When ideas affect people's lives directly, implemented by the city of Paris, they are not to be taken lightly. As Bunyard writes, what Stiegler's notion of a contributive economy shows is that what he was ultimately interested in was promoting 'good' capitalism over 'bad' capitalism, the dividing line being proletarianisation. The good and the bad, the proletarianising and the deproletarianising, are never fought by opposing capitalism. Deproletarianisation is fought from within and by working with capital. Proletarianisation is the problem, not capitalism. As Stiegler declares: 'the aim is to envisage that which is beneficial for society, as well as to the market, but in a sustainable way'.[78] Consequently, it is unclear whether there is any attempt to be found in Stiegler's work 'to put down capitalism, for good'. Instead, it is preoccupied with what to do in the meanwhile.

Solange Manche is a PhD candidate at the University of Cambridge. Her work explores the recent resurgence of the critique of political economy in contemporary French philosophy.

Notes

1. 'Bernard Stiegler: "Le capitalisme conduit à une automatisation généralisée"', interview for *Ballast*, January 3, 2019, https://www.revue-ballast.fr/bernard-stiegler-le-capitalisme-conduit-a-une-automatisation-generalisee.
2. Bernard Stiegler, *Technics and Time, 1: The Fault of Epimetheus* (Stanford: Stanford University Press, 1998), 26.
3. Bernard Stiegler, *Acting Out*, trans. David Barison, Daniel Ross and Patrick Crogan (Stanford: Stanford University Press, 2009), 31-2.
4. Ross Abbinnett, *The Thought of Bernard Stiegler: Capitalism, Technology and the Politics of Spirit* (London: Routledge, 2017), 64.
5. Bernard Stiegler, *Technics and Time, 3, Cinematic Time and the Question of Malaise*, trans. Stephen Barker (Stanford: Stanford University Press, 2011), 191-2.
6. Andreas Malm, *Fossil Capital: The Rise of Steam Power and the Roots of Global Warming* (London: Verso, 2016).
7. Tom Bunyard, 'Technoreformism', *Radical Philosophy* 174 (July/Aug 2012), 36.
8. John Hutnyk, 'Proletarianisation', *New Formations* 77 (Winter 2012), 127-49.
9. Karl Marx, *Capital: A Critique of Political Economy*, vol. 1, trans. Ben Fowkes (London: Penguin, 1990), 493. Translation amended.
10. Stiegler, *Technics and Time, 1*, 26.
11. This is absent from the parallels drawn by Bunyard, 'Technoreformism', 33-6; Benoît Dillet, 'Proletarianization, Deproletarianization and the Rise of the Amateur', *Boundary 2* 44:1 (2017), 79-105; Jason Read, *The Politics of Transindividuality* (Leiden: Brill, 2016); Shawna Vesco, 'Collective Disindividuation and/or Barbarism: Technics and Proletarianization', *Boundary 2* 42:3 (2015), 85-104.
12. Matteo Pasquinelli, 'On the Origins of Marx's General Intellect', *Radical Philosophy* 2.06 (Winter 2019), 43-56.
13. See Aaron Benanav *Automation and the Future of Work* (London: Verso, 2020) and Jason Smith, *Smart Machines and Service Work* (London: Reaktion Books, 2020).
14. Bernard Stiegler, *L'emploi est mort, vive le travail! Entretien avec Ariel Kyrou* (Paris: Mille et une nuits, 2015), 114-5.
15. Bernard Stiegler, *Automatic Society: Volume 1, The Future of Work*, trans. Daniel Ross (Cambridge: Polity Press, 2016), 25.
16. Stiegler, *Automatic Society*, 164.
17. Stiegler, *Automatic Society*, 70.
18. Victor Petit, 'Vocabulaire d'Ars Industrialis', in *Pharmacologie Du Front National* (Paris: Flammarion, 2013), 381-2.
19. Ian James, 'Bernard Stiegler and the Time of Technics', *Cultural Politics* 6:2 (2010), 207-28.
20. Bernard Stiegler, *States of Shock: Stupidity and Knowledge in the 21st Century* (Chichester: Wiley-Blackwell 2015), 157.
21. Stiegler, *Technics and Time, 3*, 16-20.
22. Stiegler, *Technics and Time, 3*, 20-1.
23. Stiegler, *Technics and Time, 1*, 245-50.
24. Petit, 'Vocabulaire d'Ars Industrialis', 381-2.
25. Gilbert Simondon, *On the Mode of Existence of Technical Objects*, trans. Cecile Malaspina and John Rogove (Minneapolis: Univocal, 2017).
26. Stiegler, *Technics and Time, 3*, 82-7.
27. Stiegler, *States of Shock*, 128. Stiegler, *États de choc : bêtise et savoir au XXIe siècle* (Paris: Mille et une nuits, 2012), 210.
28. Stiegler, *Technics and Time, 3*, 86.
29. Stiegler, *Automatic Society*, 28.
30. Eric Hobsbawm, 'Foreword', in *Karl Marx's Grundrisse: Foundations of the Critique of Political Economy 150 Years Later* (London: Routledge, 2008), xxiv.
31. See Maria Turchetto, 'From "Mass Worker" to "Empire": The Disconcerting Trajectory of Italian Operaismo', in *Critical Companion to Contemporary Marxism* (Leiden: Brill, 2007), 285. For the larger backdrop, see Razmig Keucheyan, *The Left Hemisphere: Mapping Critical Theory Today*, trans. Gregory Elliott (London: Verso, 2013), 79-85.
32. Steven Wright, *Storming Heaven: Class Composition and Struggle in Italian Autonomist Marxism* (London: Pluto, 2002), 107-114.
33. See Massimiliano Tomba and Riccardo Bellofiore, 'The "Fragment on Machines" and the Grundrisse: The Workerist Reading in Question', in Marcel van der Linden and Karl Heinz eds., *Beyond Marx: Theorising the Global Labour Relations of the Twenty-First Century*, (Leiden: Brill, 2014), 346.
34. Karl Marx, *Grundrisse* (London: Penguin, 1993), 704.

35. Wright, *Storming Heaven*, 163.
36. Antonio Negri, *La classe ouvrière contre l'état* (Paris: Éditions Galilée, 1978), 277–8. Translation my own.
37. Maurizio Lazzarato, 'Immaterial Labour', in *Radical Thought in Italy: A Potential Politics*, ed. Paolo Virno and Michael Hardt (Minneapolis: University of Minnesota Press, 1996), 133–47.
38. Lazzarato, 'Immaterial Labour', 140.
39. Compare Negri, *La classe ouvrière*, 277–8 with Antonio Negri and Michael Hardt, *Empire* (Cambridge, MA: Harvard University Press, 2000), 294.
40. Antonio Negri, *Goodbye Mr Socialism: Radical Politics in the 21st Century* (London, USA: Seven Stories, 2008), 168.
41. Isabelle Garo, *Communisme et stratégie* (Paris: Éditions Amsterdam, 2019), 126.
42. See Antoine Aubert, 'Multitudes: aux origines d'une revue radicale', *Multitudes* 3:67 (2017), 34–5.
43. Yann Moulier-Boutang, *Cognitive Capitalism* (Cambridge: Polity Press, 2011), 161–4.
44. McKenzie Wark, *A Hacker Manifesto* (Cambridge, MA: Harvard University Press, 2004), 29, 76.
45. André Gorz, *The Immaterial: Knowledge, Value and Capital*, trans. Chris Turner (London: Seagull Books, 2010), 108.
46. Gorz, *The Immaterial*, 127.
47. Stiegler, *Automatic Society*, 209–13.
48. Stiegler, *L'emploi est mort*, 36. Translation my own.
49. André Gorz, *Capitalism, Socialism, Ecology* (London: Verso, 2012), 69.
50. Frederick Harry Pitts, 'Beyond the Fragment: Postoperaismo, Postcapitalism and Marx's "Notes on Machines", 45 Years On', *Economy and Society* 46:3-4 (2017), 337.
51. Tomba and Bellofiore, 'The "Fragment on Machines"', 356.
52. Bernard Stiegler, *Économie de l'hypermatériel et psychopouvoir. Entretiens avec Philippe Petit et Vincent Bontems* (Paris: Mille et une nuits, 2008), 109–112.
53. Although Ian James argues that Stiegler's conception of historical time is anything but teleological as it does not include a notion of necessary progress, Stiegler's engagement with automation theory is another facet of his thought on technology that is undeniably teleological. See Ian James, 'Bernard Stiegler and the Time of Technics', *Cultural Politics* 6:2 (2010), 207–27.
54. Yann Moulier-Boutang, 'L'automation intellectuelle, la mort de l'emploi et le revenu de pollinisation', *Multitudes* 1:58 (2015), 17–27.
55. Kim Moody, 'High Tech, Low Growth: Robots and the Future of Work', *Historical Materialism* 26:4 (17 December 2018), 6. In fact, Stiegler never directly cites the study, but simply refers to Frey and Osborne's institutional affiliation, the University of Oxford.
56. Aaron Benanav, 'Automation and The Future of Work – I', *New Left Review* 119 (October 2019), 5–38; Benanav, 'Automation and the Future of Work – 2', *New Left Review* 120 (December 2019): 117–46; Kim Moody, 'High Tech, Low Growth: Robots and the Future of Work', *Historical Materialism* 26:4 (17 December 2018), 3–34;
57. Benanav, 'Automation and The Future of Work – I', 17.
58. Benanav, 'Automation and The Future of Work – I', 35.
59. Moody, 'High Tech, Low Growth', 16–7.
60. Smith, *Smart Machines and Service Work*, 130.
61. Pasquinelli, 'Origins of Marx's General Intellect', 45–6.
62. Lorraine Daston, 'Calculation and the Division of Labour, 1750–1950', *Bulletin of the German Historical Institute* 62 (Spring 2018), 9–30.
63. McKenzie Wark, *Capital is Dead: Is This Something Worse?* (London: Verso, 2021), 51.
64. For a good overview of the history the idea of Universal Basic Income, see Anton Jäger and Daniel Zamora, *Basic Income: An Intellectual History*, forthcoming with the University of Chicago Press, 2021. On its promotion by Musk and Zuckerberg, see Aaron Benanav, *Automation and the Future of Work* (London: Verso, 2020), 16. For progressive proposals on the Left, see Frederico Chicci and Emanuele Leonardi, 'Rethinking Basic Income', *Radical Philosophy* 2.19 (2021), 81–9.
65. Mario Tronti, 'Factory and Society', in *Workers and Capital*, trans. David Broder (London: Verso, 2019), 12–36.
66. Antonella Corsani and Maurizio Lazzarato, *Intermittents et précaires* (Paris: Éditions Amsterdam, 2008).
67. André Gorz, *Critique of Economic Reason*, trans. Gillian Handyside and Chris Turner (London: Verso, 1989), 203–8.
68. Gorz, *The Immaterial*, 122–4. Walter Van Trier, 'Do Firms Need to Be "Third Places" for Jobs to Be Good? Some Comments on André Gorz's Justification of Unconditional Income Guarantees', in *Between the Social and the Spatial: Exploring the Multiple Dimensions of Poverty and Social Exclusion*, ed. Katrien De Boyser (Ashgate: Farnham, 2009), 89–110.
69. Stiegler, *Automatic Society*, 219–21.
70. Bernard Stiegler and Ariel Kyrou, 'Le revenu contributif et le revenu universel', *Multitudes* 63:2 (July 2016), 54.
71. Stiegler, *L'emploi est mort*, 103.
72. Stiegler and Kyrou, 'Le revenu contributif et le revenu universel', 54. Translation my own.
73. *Faire de Plaine Commune un territoire d'expérimentation du revenu contributif*, a report published in 2017 by Plaine Commune addressed to M. Thierry Mandon, Minister of Higher Education and Research (2015–2017), 11.
74. Stiegler, *Automatic Society*, 215.
75. Stiegler, *L'emploi est mort*, 76–7.
76. *Faire de Plaine Commune*, 4.
77. See *Faire de Plaine Commune*, throughout.
78. Stiegler, *L'emploi est mort*, 116.

Centre for Research in Modern European Philosophy

Workshop in collaboration with the Department of Philosophy, University of Paris-8

Critique of Strategic Reason

What are the philosophical terms and repercussions of the move from centralized political organizations to social and political movements?

FRIDAY 3 DECEMBER 2021

Espace Deleuze, Université Paris 8,
2 rue de la Liberté, 93526 Saint-Denis, Paris

SPEAKERS

Éric Alliez (CRMEP/University of Paris-8)
Antonia Birnbaum (University of Paris-8)
Howard Caygill (CRMEP, Kingston University)
Peter Hallward (CRMEP, Kingston University)
Frédéric Rambeau (University of Paris-8)
Matthieu Renault (University of Paris-8)
Guillaume Silbertin-Blancs (University of Paris-8)

CRMEP BOOKS

Asserting in 1966 that 'Lenin was closer to **Max Weber**'s *Politics as Vocation* than to the German working-class struggles', the Italian radical philosopher and political theorist **Mario Tronti** set about rethinking 'the autonomy of the political'. These essays and translations of texts by Tronti reflect on the conjunctions of his thought with Max Weber's.

Contributors Howard Caygill, Alex Martin, Elettra Stimilli, Alberto Toscano, Mario Tronti (4 essays)

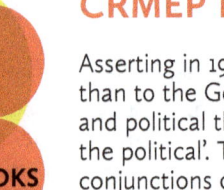

Vocations of the political
Mario Tronti & Max Weber

Thinking art
materialisms, labours, forms

Capitalism: concept, idea, image
Aspects of Marx's *Capital* today

www.kingston.ac.uk/crmep

Reviews

Android paranoia

Aaron Benanav, *Automation and the Future of Work* (London: Verso, 2020). 160pp., £12.99 hb., 978 1 83976 129 4

Jason E. Smith, *Smart Machines and Service Work: Automation in an Age of Stagnation* (London: Reaktion, 2020). 160pp., £14.95 hb., 978 1 78914 318 8

Is a future where jobs currently done by humans are carried out by robots just around the corner? Will advanced robotics, machine learning and artificial intelligence bring about a change as fundamental as the industrial revolution? Will a robot take *your* job? If you ask business page commentators, MBAs, venture capitalists, futurists, tech enthusiasts, machine learning experts, politicians, commentators, theorists and Silicon Valley CEOs, the answer is often a resounding 'yes'. Runaway technological advances, they argue, mean human labour is becoming obsolete. This obsolescence means a chance to avoid drudgery and seek out a better, more meaningful life, as long as the catastrophe of rapid-onset wage evaporation is resolved.

This vision of the future is often practically undermined by the actions of those at its centre: Silicon Valley. Take, for example, Elon Musk. In 2019, Musk promised that his company, Tesla, would have one million autonomously driven taxis on the road by the end of 2020. This did not happen. Meanwhile, an issue with Tesla's Autopilot assistive driving mode – that it is unable to decipher parked emergency vehicles – has been linked to twelve crashes since 2018. New automated technologies, it seems, promise high but fail to deliver. Perhaps the most extreme example can be found in Elizabeth Holmes' company, Theranos. Holmes claimed that she could test for hundreds of diseases with just a small pin prick's worth of blood, replacing technicians with an automated electronic process. It seemed miraculous: a means to affordable medical screening and a lucky escape for the needlephobe. Exactly *how* the testing technology worked was a closely guarded secret – intellectual property is one of the most valuable assets a Valley company produces – until the whole project collapsed when it became clear that the technology simply did not exist. Theranos' unravelling left many in the lurch: patients who had been misdiagnosed, funders who had given $700m to the company and the retailer, Walgreens, which had opened forty Theranos Wellness Centres inside its stores. What seemed like the future of medical technology turned out to be an embarrassing failure.

Nevertheless, the automation proponents believe that we are on the threshold of a new era in which brilliant machines, unhindered by the fleshy externalities of workers displace human labour. Jobs can and will be replaced: the technologically possible becomes the probable. To solve the 'jobs-apocalypse' scenario of mass technological unemployment many automation proponents argue for a Universal Basic Income, a proposal explored by Andrew Yang, Martin Ford and Daniel Susskind, among others. A leftist version of the automation thesis, often as much a provocation to imagine an end to drudgery as prediction about a concrete future, can be found in Alex Williams and Nick Srnicek's *Inventing the Future* (2015) and Aaron Bastani's *Fully Automated Luxury Communism* (2018).

The future is hard to predict. Alongside the question of whether the automated future is a utopia or a nightmare, there are disagreements about the pace and depth of change: will automation substitute human labour, or merely augment it? Where automation supporters converge is that the developments that make a computerised future possible are already underway and that the barriers to their fulfilment are primarily technological and temporal. It is into this debate that two new books, Aaron Benanav's *Automation and the Future of Work* and

Jason E. Smith's *Smart Machines and Service Work*, seek to intervene.

Even the most breathless techno-optimists are aware that there remain profound technological barriers to completely substituting human labour – Erik Brynjolfsson and Andrew McAfee, for example, note that robots are typically less dexterous and agile than humans. But Smith and Benanav are not so bothered about the technical limitations of new and developing technology (though they do note that these remain rather significant barriers to full automation) as much as the economic conditions that render automation, of the kind its proponents claim is fast-approaching, unlikely. Both books are relatively short – *Automation and the Future of Work* reaches a slim 99 pages, *Smart Machines and Service Work* stands at 149 – but gather significant cold water to pour on automation's fever dreams. Rather than being on the tipping point of a new digital age, one already starting to renew sluggish productivity rates, we are, they both argue, beset by a profound economic stagnation. This stagnation means that runaway productivity increases predicted by automation proponents are not happening, and are extremely unlikely to happen, because of a profound economic crisis that goes beyond a few bad business cycles. Both locate this stagnation in a crisis of profitability. Benanav pins it to Robert Brenner's notion of a 'long downturn' (Brenner was one of his doctoral supervisors at the University of California). Benanav's target is what he terms the 'automation discourse'. This is a consensus straddling the political left, right and centre, which holds that mass technological unemployment is a fast-approaching horizon, offering, should it be managed correctly, a chance to enter a world of abundance and leisure. He argues that while technological changes may well displace or transform some jobs in the future, the idea that technology is already destroying jobs and expelling large numbers of workers from employment is false. This long downturn begins, Brenner and Benanav argue, with post-war developments in manufacturing generating global overcapacity as more efficient manufacturing suppliers joined the world market, but less efficient suppliers did not exit. This results in a disincentive for firms to invest, eventually dragging on GDP growth. As Benanav puts it, '[d]ecades of industrial overcapacity killed the manufacturing growth engine, and no alternative to it has been found'. Manufacturing output rates slowed and the engine of economic growth falls out of the car at the national and global scale.

For Smith, the crisis has its roots in the expansion of unproductive (in the Marxist sense) labour. As companies compete, they seek to gain a competitive edge against their rivals using labour-saving technology. This reduces the total amount of labour involved in the process, meaning profitability stagnates. Employers are able to draw on a growing reserve army of labour, permitting greater exploitation of that workforce and creating another barrier to automating tasks in new sectors. Value-producing work tends to be increasingly concentrated and distribution more diffuse. 'This pattern', he argues, 'in which enormous productive gains through economies of scale at the point of production are offset by the more labour intensive activities in the circulation process, appears to be a global feature of global capitalist production'. To demonstrate this, he analyses a typical consumer good (or at least a typical American consumer good) – an air-conditioning unit – standing in for Marx's linen coat. 80% of the world's air conditioning units are made in China, and one third of all residential units are made by just one company, Gree. These units are then shipped and sold in small, spatially dispersed retail outlets. Thus, the ratio of unproductive to productive labour grows. This stagnation is the true cause of a key piece of evidence used by automation proponents: low demand for labour. Automation theorists, then, would be wrong to assign the cause of the persistent low demand for labour to technological innovation displacing workers. Whatever its precise cause, the symptoms of stagnation they describe are similar: firms are hesitant to take risks and instead shore up their existing position by using available cash to buy back shares, along with sweating or firing workers. This dynamic comes across particularly clearly in Smith's analysis of share buybacks: between 2015 and 2017, he notes, American corporations spent $3 out of every $5 of their net profit on stock repurchases. Firms are speculative platforms, gobbling up competitors or indebted 'zombies' attached to a life support of cheap credit.

If technological change were really displacing workers, as automation theorists claim, productivity would be increasing. But, as Robert Solow pithily put it, computers are seen everywhere except the productivity statistics. The automation theorists, then, are wrong on the dynamics of the economy. But might they be correct about its future trajectory? Again, there is strong evidence presented in both books to doubt this. Dwindling returns and access to a low-wage and easily exploited workforce mean that companies might not be particularly interested in investing in new technologies. Even if there were investment, Benanav argues, such '[p]rofit-driven technological advances are highly unlikely to overcome human drudgery as such' because of the enduring presence of cheap, exploitable labour. Moreover, Smith suggests, automation tends to impact sectors of the economy, rather than the economy as a whole, with workers displaced from the automated car industry ending up pooling in low-wage and low-skill sectors like logistics. This further disincentivises automation in those sectors. In Smith's view, a wage society is not one in which full automation can prevail. A further barrier is that the areas automation would need to traverse before the whole gamut of work was automated is activity that is 'low-skill' for human workers but extremely difficult for machines. Smith points out that today's 'low-skill' labour often relies on unpredictable, highly intuitive and highly relational decisions and tasks, rather than the routine processes of an assembly line. The challenges to the automation of such work are profound.

The jobs-apocalypse scenario in which each job is replaced with its automated version is a bit of an easy target. It is extremely unlikely to come to pass. Previous bouts of unemployment have demonstrably proven this to be a rare development. Instead, local expulsions from skilled work and the reorganisation and deskilling of that work are typical. Technological developments tend to reorganise rather than fully replace human work. Both books, however, give readers good reason to doubt the pace and trajectory of technological change even if it does not substitute for individual jobs. By showing that automation cheerleaders have it wrong about the contemporary economy, and that their glorious predictions are unlikely to materialise, Smith and Benanav are able to puncture their vision of the future.

The future, though, remains bleak. Its bleakness is unlikely to come from technological unemployment, but rather, a combination of low demand for labour meaning underemployment, and potentially of expulsions of workers from a shrinking formal sector. As Phil Jones has persuasively argued, workers might be dispersed into 'digital piecework' – miniscule tasks of data labelling, paid well below subsistence rates – as well as the growing 'servant economy'. Where technology develops, it most likely will be in the service of profit and the sweating of labour rather than its liberation.

How might such a future be resisted? Given that the present is profoundly troubling – secular stagnation, exploitative and undignified jobs, cruel management practices – what should take its place and who should do the taking? Both authors identify agents for change. Benanav looks hopefully at social struggles since the 2008 global financial crisis and their tactics of stoppages, occupations and blockades. A declining share of manufacturing in total employment, he notes, 'means that these workers no longer have the capacity to cast themselves as representatives of a more just and rational future order' and that emergent struggles are 'unlikely to look like the labour movements of earlier centuries'. Lean supply chains, he argues, offer a chance for workers outside the point of production to have leverage through blocking circulation.

Similarly, Smith, following James Boggs, suggests that 'outsiders' – those expelled from formal work – might have a crucial role to play in struggle. He is more circumspect about the challenges such movements face: the isolation of workers is a formidable barrier. The workers movement, he argues, was at 'once product and the reflection' of industrial production. The working class becomes an organised mass, concentrated in large workplaces, it goes through what Marx and Engels describe as 'the stern schooling of labour'. By contrast, a deepening 'servant economy' fragments workers into smaller, isolated workplaces. Smith considers how a worker's place in the social division of labour and in the specialisation of production offer different openings for action. Successful teachers' strikes, for example, have been able to use their specific place in the social division of labour – their work is a precondition for those with children being able to go to work. They cannot be offshored or automated and when their work stops, other work does too. Workers in technologically progressive sectors have power too, in their case, by dint of their place in the technical division of labour. But retail, restaurant, care workers and other similar sectors, characterised by low wage relation work, do not have a decisive position in either division of labour. For such workers, 'none of the conditions favouring a "coming upsurge" prevail'.

Both authors argue for the difficult but fundamentally important task of building power for those who must work to live in conditions of diminishing demand for labour. Benanav goes beyond the identification of agents by which and around whom this power can be rebuilt in a chapter considering what he terms 'silver bullets' – 'one quick trick' solutions to secular stagnation. He presents and discards one potential way out – the path of Keynesian stimulus. Whether his calculation here is correct depends upon two claims: is he right about the limited growth returns of stimulus spending since the 1970s, and is stagnation so profound as to be resistant to all attempts at reinvigoration? On both counts, there may be reasons to be doubtful. As Alexis Moraitis and Jack Copley argue, 'debt-fuelled spending was *not* channelled into enhancing ordinary people's consuming power and thereby directly boosting demand'. On the latter point, they wonder if 'industrial overcapacity is necessarily impervious to states' attempts to regulate competition, plan investment or directly stimulate demand.'

A second 'silver bullet' discussed and dismissed is that of Universal Basic Income. UBI is often presented as the cure to the jobs-apocalypse. Benanav provides a brief history of UBI – from Thomas Paine's lump sum payment for all adults, via Friedrich Hayek and Milton Friedman, to Phillipe Van Parijs and Charles Murray. He considers its liberal, leftist and right-wing variations. The care taken with this history is commendable, especially when criticisms of UBI often tend toward bad faith. One recurrent example is the claim that because UBI has been proposed by neoliberals and even outright racists that its support from the left is inappropriate. Kathi Weeks – a supporter of UBI – has termed this the 'strange bedfellows' argument. It is mostly hogwash. Two disparate and distinct traditions can converge on a policy proposal, especially one that they understand quite differently, without undermining either of their own cases for it. Instead of taking cheap shots, Benanav considers what is valuable about UBI and why it might be appealing, singling out the goal of *universal* provision as justice-driven reparatory policy, especially important 'in a country like the United States, where racism birthed welfare programs that treat the poor with suspicion, if not contempt'.

But UBI – of the left-wing variety – is ruled out on practical grounds. Firstly, Benanav calls into question the faith that leftist UBI advocates have in its ability to repair communities and support the scaling of movements and unions. This is partly justified: there is certainly a tendency on the part of advocates for more free time or a UBI to imagine that people will put their time to worthy use – certainly not a given. This tendency is taken to task in Mareile Pfannebecker and James A. Smith's *Work Want Work* (2020). However, many advocates of UBI are what might be dubbed "yes *and*" advocates of the policy. If it has potential for (re)building working class power, it is only when bundled with other reforms, like 'Universal Basic Services', or fighting regressive anti-trade union legislation. 'UBI-first' proposals, which pin emancipation to UBI alone, are, as Orlando Lazar argues, unlikely to succeed. The second practical ground for discarding UBI is that it does not strike at a crucial weapon that capital possesses – *capital strike* – disinvestment and capital flight. The only way, Benanav argues, to achieve change is to take control of that weapon.

Benanav then describes a new way of imagining a future utopia: fully-rounded humanistic production and the establishment of shared abundance. This is a compelling vision. His vision of the future can function in a similar way to that which Helen Hester and Will Stronge see as the role for utopias: a 'vector rather than terminus'. Refiguring abundance as a social relation – a shared world of public goods, with no possibility of excluding anyone from them, is a helpful corrective to the sometimes overblown account of luxury as a threshold in some left automation theorists (Aaron Bastani, for example, claims that we could all lead lives like today's billionaires). This vision should orient, he argues, new social struggles, pushing them toward what he terms 'the conquest of production'. A conquest of production might be the only way to deactivate capital strike but if UBI and Keynesian stimulus can be discarded on the basis of practicality, would not this highly desirable but challenging proposal fail on the same terms? That said, there are certainly compelling reasons to favour this vision of cooperative justice, work redistribution and shared abundance that are normative rather than practical.

Both Benanav and Smith take up the role of the sceptic. Their work suggests that to be a good sceptic involves going beyond the principle of charity to see *why* ideas might appeal to others even when the sceptic finds them wanting. Smith approaches a conceptually complex field and prises apart elisions and confusions with deftness. Benanav's automation scepticism is all the more convincing for its partially submerged ambivalence: he describes his response to automationists' vision of their future as a way to develop his own, 'which by comparison with theirs was still full of the dullest-possible grey'. This ambivalence is productive; it enables an experiment in thinking otherwise. Benanav and Smith, as good sceptics, do not merely cast doubt but offer new hope.

Amelia Horgan

Violence, justice and justification

Judith Butler, *The Force of Non-Violence: An Ethico-Political Bind* (London: Verso, 2020). 224pp., £14.99 hb., 978 1 78873 276 5.

Elizabeth Frazer and Kimberly Hutchings, *Can Political Violence Ever Be Justified?* (Cambridge: Polity, 2019). 140pp., £35.00 hb., £9.99 pb., 978 1 50952 920 9 hb., 978 1 50952 921 6 pb..

Adriana Cavarero with Judith Bulter and Bonnie Honig, *Towards a Feminist Ethics of Nonviolence* (New York: Fordham University Press, 2021). 192pp, £72.00 hb., £18.99 pb., 978 0 82329 008 6 hb., 978 0 82329 009 3 pb..

Jericho Brown begins his poem 'Bullet Points' with a vow:

> I will not shoot myself
> In the head, and I will not shoot myself
> In the back ... and if I do,
> I promise you, I will not do it
> In a police car while handcuffed

His 2019 collection *The Tradition* comes back time and time again to the ways in which bodies are opened up to violence. Frequently, the lethal agent is the state. But not always. Later in 'Bullet Points', Brown's narrator describes other, more quotidian pressures that waste lives with the same finality as a cop's revolver:

> When I kill me, I will
> Do it the same way most Americans do,
> I promise you ... so broke I freeze
> In one of these winters we keep
> Calling worst.

That police power, white supremacy and capital focus their collective attention on the same bodies is not a coincidence, of course. Yet although 'Bullet Points' depicts these forces shaping and ending lives with catastrophic immediacy, there remains something slippery and elusive about the violence they wield. The acts of coercive force that the poem describes reshape and deform their wider social terrain, making protectors out of murderers and shooters out of the shot. As a consequence, Brown's narrator often struggles to locate their centre, map their trajectory and point of origin, or identify the vulnerabilities that they exploit. Even grief must be accounted for within parameters set by the same institutions that make mourning necessary in the first place ('He took/Me from us and left my body, which is .../Greater than the settlement/A city can pay a mother to stop crying').

In May 2020, *The Tradition* won the Pulitzer Prize for poetry. Less than three weeks later, Derek Chauvin murdered George Floyd ('I promise if you hear/Of me dead anywhere near/A cop, then that cop killed me'), and the streets erupted. Like 'Bullet Points', last summer's global wave of protest often foregrounded specific instances of violence, but never at the expense of the wider ideological and socio-economic formations that enabled them. Their varied diagnoses and demands stemmed from a recognition that racism and white supremacy are not exceptional, but rather structure our worlds in ways that cut untidily across the scalar categories of 'local', 'national' and 'global'. The political calls that resulted – for police and prison abolition, for a full reckoning with the legacies of slavery and colonialism, for open borders, and much else besides – matched the scope of this critique.

To resist and dismantle these formidable institutions requires acknowledging what Audre Lorde described as the 'atavistic fear of an articulated power that is not on your terms'. Lorde was speaking about the 1973 case of Thomas Shea, an undercover NYPD cop who shot and killed ten year old Clifford Glover in Queens, New York City. The jury who acquitted Shea of murder contained a single Black woman and eleven white men. In an interview with Adrienne Rich, Lorde imagined herself in that woman's position. 'How do you take a position against them? How do you reach down into threatening difference without being killed – or killing?' How, in short, do you challenge a system sustained by and saturated with violence without opening up yourself (or others) to injury or death?

Many theorists, revolutionaries and activists have approached the problems of coalition-building, collective agency and structural transformation by advocating programmes of political violence. For some, it offers the surest way of undoing existing hierarchies and injustices, while for others it provides a crucible in which new identities and subjectivities can be formed. Both positions are predicated on the belief that facing down 'an articulated power that is not on your terms' justifies and perhaps even necessitates the use of force. Yet Lorde's challenge is not just to 'reach down into threatening difference', but to do so 'without being killed – *or killing*'.

Three recent books have taken up Lorde's problem, though they approach it from different directions and with different purposes in mind. In *Can Political Violence Ever Be Justified?*, political theorists Elizabeth Frazer and Kimberly Hutchings outline many of the arguments that have been deployed in order to condone or legitimise political violence. Frazer and Hutchings' discussion of these justificatory schemes and strategies is animated by a keen awareness of the difficulty of pinning down precisely what violence is and how it relates to politics. Does the state practice 'political violence', or does it merely exercise 'legitimate force'? If the former, then to what extent are the violent actions of those who exercise the sovereign's authority and will theirs? Is Derek Chauvin's unyielding knee his own, or is it the embodiment of a foundationally racist state and its murderous policing practices? Can it be both? If so, then where is the boundary between 'political violence' and criminality, if one can even be traced at all? And how might 'good' or 'legitimate' instances of violence be distinguished from their opposite?

Any attempt to justify political violence must work with ambiguities like these, yet as Frazer and Hutchings rightly note, violence is often taken for granted as a surgical instrument to be raised or set down as circumstances dictate. The right to self-defence, for example, presumes that one can take up arms in order to neutralise an external threat to one's self, one's family or one's property. Once the balance of social order has been restored, one simply puts away one's musket, pours out a glass and pulls a rocking chair out onto the verandah. Of course, self-defence has always been a 'right' from which certain (racialised, gendered, otherwise unruly) bodies are excluded, as Elsa Dorlin has pointed out in these pages (*RP* 2.05) and elsewhere. Even taking self-defence on its own terms, however, it must be acknowledged that social threats are not merely physical, and neither do they necessarily result from instability or breakdown. The measures taken to address them, moreover, cannot be considered independently from the orders they preserve, maintain or restore.

If violence and politics are not mutually exclusive categories, then one cannot distinguish between acceptable and unacceptable instances of political violence using arguments that (for example) disaggregate society into a collection of rights-bearing individuals. Instead, violence is justifiable insofar as it is 'necessary', a broad category that encompasses Machiavelli's insistence that political *virtù* can manifest itself in acts of cruelty, as well as Fanon's embrace of violence's creative possibility in a world in which the selfhood of the colonised is systematically denied. As Frazer and Hutchings note, however, Fanon also recognised violence as a force that generated extraordinary psychological strain and trauma among victims and perpetrators alike. It is precisely for this reason that its logic is so difficult to escape: if violence is simultaneously creative and destructive, then even instances that are apparently 'justifiable' are liable to fracture or even destroy the subjectivities they bring into being.

This sense of violence's ambivalence informs Frazer and Hutchings' turn to feminist theory in order to argue that 'our ethical and political attention should be on the world that violence instantiates, as opposed to the world it is supposed to produce'. Because there is something overwhelming about violence, something difficult if not impossible to contain, 'the world that violence instantiates' is one that threatens not just this or that subject but also the intersubjective relations that sustain politics itself as a field of human activity. Political violence, they conclude, is thus wholly *un*justifiable: it is predicated on an acceptance that some subjects can rightfully harm others, who must implicitly or explicitly be abjected altogether from the political field. It turns out to be a commitment 'to something that cannot be made right'.

Can Political Violence Ever Be Justified? engages generously and insightfully with a wide range of theorists of political violence, and does so concisely and accessibly. While acknowledging that a short text of little over a hundred pages will inevitably be limited in scope, however, two omissions nevertheless stand out. The first is any substantive discussion of theories of non-violence, or what a politics founded on non-violent principles might look like. Frazer and Hutchings speak with clarity and conviction about the limitations of theories of political violence, but their conclusion that 'the ways in which political violence has been justified now and in the past fail, and that political violence can never be justified' raises questions about non-violence that the book gestures towards without fully addressing.

The second concerns the role 'justification' as a discursive strategy plays in the practice of political violence. Frazer and Hutchings acknowledge the openness of their key terms, and make clear that 'violence', 'political violence' and 'justification' are not only contested terms in their own right, but also condition each others' meanings. Nevertheless, their critique largely focuses on the relationship between 'politics' and 'violence': political violence can never be justified because violence destroys the capacity for collective flourishing on which politics depends; it 'unmakes the world', to paraphrase Elaine Scarry. As such, political violence is something that falls apart under the weight of its own contradictions.

What, then, of justification? Frazer and Hutchings argue that justifications of political violence often form 'part of [its] enabling conditions', masking or legitimising its destructive tendencies in the name of values such as 'order', 'justice' and 'self-preservation'. Yet despite this, their argument remains animated by justificatory modes of critical judgement. Does their focus on violence 'as it is practiced and experienced' necessarily loosen justification from the discourses of permission and enablement that so often define it? The martial reveries of someone like Filippo Marinetti suggest otherwise: there can be joy in cruelty, in harm, even in slaughter. Instead, might their argument point towards a rejection of justification as a framework for thinking about political violence altogether?

One text that Frazer and Hutchings do not cite that kept coming to mind as I read *Can Political Violence Ever Be Justified?* is Walter Benjamin's 'Critique of Violence'. Among Benjamin's arguments is that the legal, political and ethical frameworks through which actions are constituted as 'just' or 'unjust' are themselves founded upon and formed through violence, and cannot be conceived separately from it. In their new book *The Force of Nonviolence*, Judith Butler frames Benjamin's problem as follows: 'if we only think about violence within the framework of its possible justification or lack of justification, does that framework not determine the phenomenon of violence in advance?'

Butler shows how justifications of violence often produce a sort of semantic confusion. Violence is often justified on the grounds that it is *not* violent: that it is in fact responding to violence, or to the threat of violence as exemplified by particular assemblies or bodies that prefigure (or are said to prefigure) threat, harm or disorder. Justification is here an instrument of violence; a way of constructing the (racialised, gendered) threats that underpin its legitimacy. 'If a demonstration in support of freedom of expression', Butler writes, 'a demonstration that exercises that very freedom, is called "violent", that can only be because the power that misuses language that way seeks to secure its own monopoly on violence through maligning the opposition'.

One consequence of this dissimulation of violence as 'security', 'law-enforcement' or simply what it takes to maintain 'order' is that non-violence itself gets dragged into the semantic swirl. How can non-violence serve as a framework for action in a context where the indiscriminate firing of rubber bullets and tear gas constitutes 'keeping the peace'? To think about violence primarily in terms of its justification (or lack thereof) does not appear to provide an obvious way out of this mire. Instead, Butler starts with ontology: 'there is a sense in which violence done to another is at once a violence done to the self', and that 'nonviolence ... [is] a way of acknowledging that social relation, however fraught it may be'. In this sense, non-violence is prefigurative and performative: it is practiced in order to 'lay open the possibilities that belong to a newer political imaginary'. It also implicitly refuses to be restrained within a framework that sees commitment as a matter of conscience – how can it be, given the opposition between the individualism of this position and the relationality that underpins non-violence as Butler sees it?

For Butler, a commitment to non-violence that derives from an acknowledgment of our ontological interdependence simultaneously demands a recognition of our equality. Because we are all formed in relations of dependence that continue to sustain and nourish us throughout our lives, none of us can claim precedence over any other. As in much of their work over the past fifteen years, Butler conceives of this equality in terms of grievability: lives are valued insofar as they are grievable, and violence emerges when lives are valued differentially or stripped of their value altogether, when the hypothetical or actual loss of this or that life is no longer rendered *as a loss*. Conversely, to practice an ethic of non-violence is to affirm the equal grievability of all lives, with that equality rooted not in the atomised terms of liberal humanism but rather in interdependence.

Crucially, this vision of equality is not a vision of harmony. To conceive of our selves as constructed by and sustained through interaction with others does not presume relations of peace or concord. Non-violence, as Butler's title suggests, is a *forceful* commitment. And indeed, the lack of self-sufficiency that defines the dependent subject is for Butler a source of deep anxiety, yearning, fear and even rage. The potential for conflict that arises from our sociality cannot be finally overcome: to repress or prohibit violent impulses is simply to internalise them. Instead, Butler relocates the psychic impulses that undergird violence, and that stem from the relational subject's inexorable incompleteness, within a 'counter-institutional ethos and practice' that seeks to preserve and maintain our relational obligations to one another.

In order to perform this act of recontextualisation, Butler turns to psychoanalysis. This framework allows her to foreground the ways violence not only produces fractured and divided subjective and intersubjective spaces, but also emerges from them. Like Jacqueline Rose, in her recent *On Violence and On Violence Against Women* (2021), Butler uses Freud in tandem with his feminist interlocutors and critics in order to show how violence often functions as a desperate flail against our incapacity to shore up our selves. The demand non-violence makes upon the subject is to live and act *with* this incompleteness, without projecting aggression outwards onto 'phantasms' constructed in order to provide an externalised threat to one's imagined wholeness. For this reason, an ethic and/or politics of non-violence has to begin with a critique of violence: it must 'confront all these phantasmagoric and political challenges', and by refusing their lure carve open a new intersubjective space in which they no longer hold sway. It manifests an 'insurrectionary solidarity' that is forceful by virtue of its persistence in the face of forces that would otherwise overwhelm it.

Butler's argument both builds on and contributes to a wider feminist literature concerned with developing ways of social and political living that stem from a relational understanding of the self. At the heart of this literature sits the work of Adriana Cavarero, with whom Butler acknowledges an affinity in their contribution to *Towards a Feminist Ethics of Nonviolence*, a symposium on Cavarero's work that also features reflections by Bonnie Honig (among others), as well as an essay by Cavarero herself. For Cavarero, western philosophy is founded upon a fictionally 'upright' thinking subject, with its guiding metaphor to be found in Plato's cave, whose prisoners' procession to enlightenment commences with them standing up. In contrast, Cavarero posits an ethics of 'inclination' in which the self is always leaning outwards, away from its internal centre of gravity. Unexpectedly, Cavarero's model for this posture is a vision of motherhood, namely Leonardo da Vinci's *Virgin and Child with St Anne*. It is here that both Butler and Honig intervene, with the former conceiving of inclination in queer terms as something that haunts rectitude as its constitutive other side, and the latter building on the radical re-reading of Sophocles that she developed in *Antigone, Interrupted* (2013) by suggesting sorority rather than maternity as an alternative model for feminist relationality.

While accepting Butler and Cavarero's relational ontology, however, questions still remain about the ethical and political demands that are made when violence is unleashed not only on ontologically related selves but also on bodies in their spatio-temporal ipseity. In a manner reminiscent of Michel Serres' writings on skin in *The Five Senses*, Butler takes the body to be 'the threshold of the person, the site of passage and porosity, the evidence of an openness to alterity that is definitional of the body itself'. Yet even if the individualised body provides an insufficient account of personhood, it is still a necessary condition of any person's life. At moments when it is physically threatened, there is rarely space for the articulation of critique: by the time the knee is pressing down upon the trachea in the name of this or that phantasmatic threat, relationality has already fractured beyond repair. While Butler is surely right to argue, with Cavarero, that 'there is no sustaining of singularity outside the context of constitutive sociality and ecology', the act of extinguishing a body's claim to life is one with singular as well as social consequences. What form can non-violence's 'open-ended struggle with violence and its countervailing forces' take in these moments of immediate existential danger?

It is clear that responding to this question cannot entail relapsing into the atomistic individualism that underpins justificatory discourses of 'self-defence'. The presumption that the subject stands autonomously is, as Butler and Cavarero both note, a masculinist fiction. Yet they as well as Frazer and Hutchings are clear that non-violence does not entail submission – quite the opposite, in fact. Are we left where we began, at Lorde's crossroads, facing down 'an articulated power that is not on our terms'? Perhaps. But non-violence is not a panacea; it cannot transcend the crises violence brings about, whether ethical, political, or existential. Instead, it begins to build a world where such crises might never come to pass; a world it is necessary to work towards, because – as Jericho Brown tells us in his 2014 collection *The New Testament* – 'nothing we erect is our own'.

Alister Wedderburn

Abstract egalitarianism

Katrina Forrester, *In the Shadow of Justice: Postwar Liberalism and the Remaking of Political Philosophy* (Princeton: Princeton University Press, 2019). 432pp., £28.00 hb., 978 0 69116 308 6

In 1952, a young American philosopher named John Rawls arrived in Oxford on a Fulbright scholarship. Fresh from military service in the Pacific that had diverted his earlier ambitions of becoming an Episcopalian priest, he was redirecting his prodigious energies towards questions philosophical and political, spending his time discussing logic and language with analytic philosophers and talking politics with the anxiously anti-Stalinist revisionist wing of the British Labour Party. The ideas he first discussed in post-war Oxford remained on his mind, surfacing occasionally in eagerly circulated, unpublished papers until in 1971, the same year that the collapse of the Bretton-Woods system heralded the advent of a new economic order, the book he had been writing was finally published. It was called *A Theory of Justice,* and, in the following years and decades, the doctrine of 'liberal egalitarianism', expounded in five hundred pages of densely argued prose, would come to set the terms of debate in Anglophone political philosophy. It determined the kind of questions that could be asked and the forms that acceptable answers might take. Political philosophy, by and large, would take place under the long shadow cast by Rawls' book. Katerina Forrester's *In The Shadow of Justice* is the most comprehensive and impressive attempt to historicise liberal egalitarianism, defamiliarising its near-hegemonic conclusions and denaturalising its assumptions, and thereby asking what might emerge from out of its shadow.

Forrester's book is an intellectual history of liberal egalitarianism, but it does not dwell on the various streams of influence that went into Rawl's book, instead examining in detail its legacy, and the ways that the evolution of the doctrine overlapped with the political and philosophical developments of the late twentieth century.

Though a work of political philosophy, Forrester spends less time pouring over the minutiae of Rawls' texts and focuses instead on examining the successes and failures of this particular political philosophy as it made (or failed to make) contact with political reality. She is clear that there is still much in Rawls that can be drawn on today. By separating what is living from what is dead in Rawls' philosophy, it might 'be put to radical ends and admit a more demanding egalitarianism than he might himself have advocated'.

In terms of philosophy, Rawls' book arrived in the right place at the right time. In the wake of concentration camps and the atom bomb, a generation of British and American philosophers had grown dissatisfied with the reigning non-cognitivism that reduced the study of ethics to the study of the logic of ethical language; they were seeking instead a framework for substantial moral and political theorising. Bernard Williams, a philosopher who would later come to have grave doubts about Rawls' project, spoke for many when he declared in an early review that *A Theory of Justice* was 'not merely a great achievement of intelligence and moral reflection ... but also notably heartening'. Heartening in that it gave a generation of Anglo-American philosophers a new faith in the ability of philosophy not only to pose axiological questions but also to attempt to answer them, in order to find some moral grounds for the politics of a world emerging from the ashes.

If it was in part this metaphilosophical ambition, the reconceptualisation of what political philosophy was and what it might do, that inspired Rawls' contemporaries, its moral vision and conceptual clarity accounted for its continued influence. Liberal egalitarianism, the doctrine expounded in *A Theory of Justice*, offered an unapologetically moral account of the 'basic structure' of a just society (roughly the set of interrelated institutions that would ensure 'justice as fairness'), offering to marry the demands of liberty and of equality in a revivified version of the social contract tradition. Conceptually, the theory begins with the 'original position', a kind of thought experiment where individuals are tasked with deciding on the basic structure of a society from behind a 'veil of ignorance', deprived of any knowledge of who exactly they would be in this society – whether they would be rich or poor, white or black, male or female. The device is intended on the one hand to ensure liberty (for surely nobody would consent in advance to a system that would infringe on their freedoms) and equality (for surely we would not set up an unequal system if we might find ourselves at the bottom of this system when the veil is lifted). Liberal egalitarianism, in its grand ambition, begins in abstraction: behind a veil, outside of history.

The major question an intellectual history of liberal egalitarianism must ask is why a theory concerned with the basic structure of a just society, and with the equitable distribution of resources, becomes intellectually dominant not in the post-war era that at least paid lip service to these ideals, but in the era of rampant market-driven ideology that succeeded it, dismissing its ideals as fantasy. In other words, why did liberal egalitarianism achieve its near total ascendency only after the rise of neoliberal politics made a liberal philosophy with a distributive, market-correcting stance seem an appealing and moral corrective?

One answer, suggested by Raymond Geuss, is that liberal egalitarianism is simply a legitimating ideology. Liberal egalitarianism was a 'compensatory fantasy' for left-liberals who had lost political power but continued to hold on to an idealisation of post-war social democracy – a sophisticated, elegant normative system through which to view and appraise the world from the comfort of a Harvard study, rather than a tool to change it. Its untimeliness thus reveals a deeply flawed attitude to the relation between politics and philosophy, theory and praxis: liberal egalitarianism can serve as a compensatory fantasy only because liberal egalitarians (Rawls himself, first and foremost, but also his followers: T.M. Scanlon, Ronald Dworkin, Thomas Nagel, Michael Walzer) never had a genuine ambition of using the theory to inspire social change.

Forrester's book provides a more historically detailed, more even-handed development of this historicist critique of liberal egalitarianism. For Forrester, to tell the story of the untimeliness of liberal egalitarianism in the twentieth century is to tell a 'ghost story' – to trace the way in which Rawls' theory was 'haunted by the ghosts of postwar liberalism', its attempts to speak to contemporary political issues compromised by ideas drawn from its own historical conditions of possibility, long since passed, ideas which 'exerted a destabilising pull on the present'. Forrester demonstrates that the problem was not, as Geuss seems to suggest, that liberal egalitarians were simply uninterested in political reality. She points out that Rawls and his successors were at times hyper-attuned to what came to be called the 'public affairs' of the day, almost as if to forestall objections of irrelevance and detachment. *In the Shadow of Justice* is structured around some of these philosophical responses to political events: the chapter entitled 'Obligations' shows how the civil rights movement and student protests against Vietnam prompted Rawls to integrate an account of civil disobedience into *A Theory of Justice*; 'Going Global' examines how liberal egalitarians responded to new postcolonial questions of global justice by attempting to expand the notion of 'basic structure' to the planetary level; 'The Problem of the Future' how, in response to the growing awareness of climate change, Rawlsian philosophers sought to extend the notion of 'person' so central to Rawls' liberal contract theory so as to include future generations.

Many of these adjustments to the theory were ingenious – one thing the reader never doubts is the intellectual sophistication of Rawls and his followers – but one of Forrester's most remarkable observations is that, even in the original 1971 text, attempts to 'apply' liberal egalitarianism to the problems of the day relied, knowingly or not, on an institutional order that was *already* hopelessly idealised, hopelessly distant, or both. Take Rawls' fundamental belief in consensus, in the idea that 'deep down, social life rested on the possibility of consensus and ethical agreement'. Forrester contends that the elegant abstractions of the basic structure, and the preference for 'ideal theory', made it impossible for Rawls to realise that one of its most fundamental premises 'idealised a moment from the mid-century American past when liberalism was triumphant against right and left', a moment that had already passed by the time of the book's publication, and from which we are distantly estranged today.

The capacious, flexible and abstract nature of Rawls' theory allowed it to absorb the impact of just about any political shocks, both the sharp shocks of war and civil disorder and the slow, triumphal march of free-market fundamentalism. This was due in part to the broad and fundamental nature of the theory – empirical claims and disagreements about strategy could be shrugged off as 'merely incidental' problems, whilst the really basic claims were abstract, or vague, enough to remain largely unchallenged – and because, after half a decade of institutional dominance, liberal egalitarianism appeared to have neutralised its major theoretical opponents. Forrester convincingly argues that the eventual hegemony of

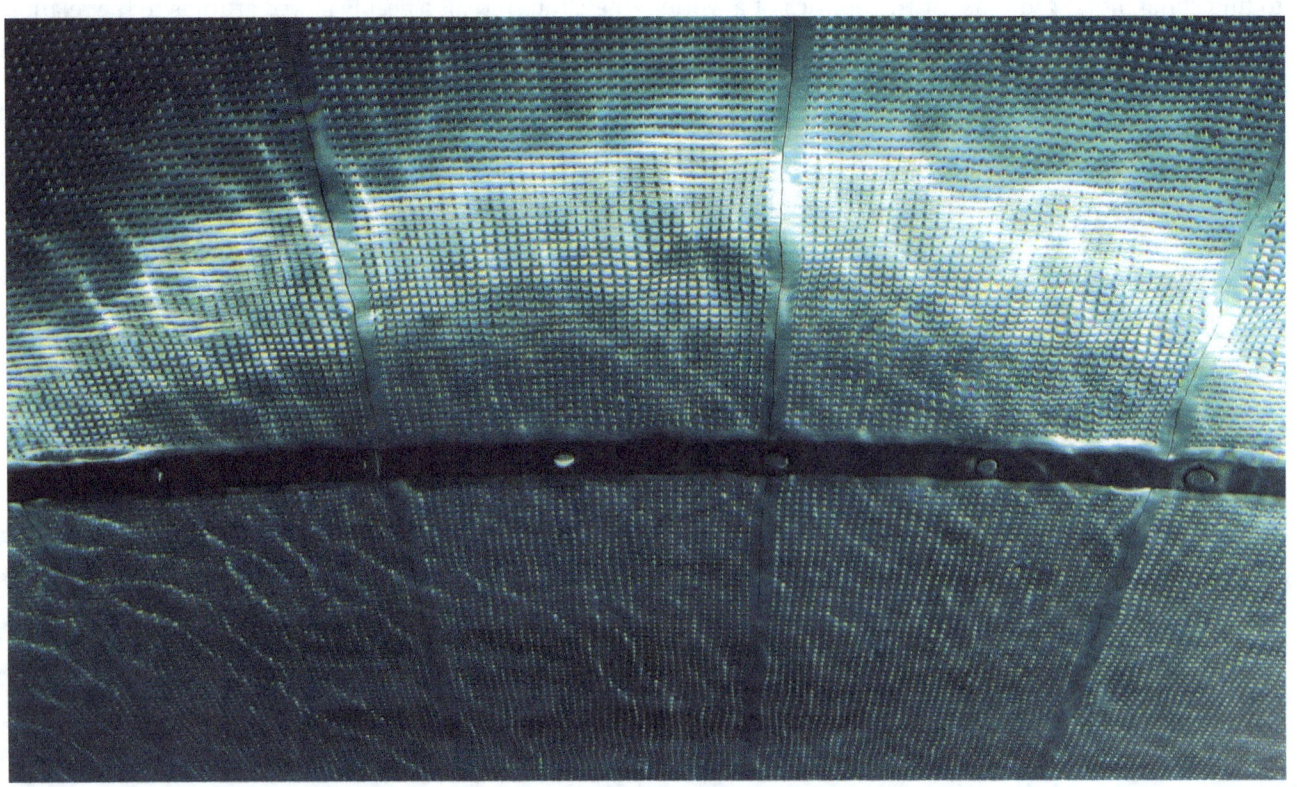

liberal egalitarianism lay just as much in domesticating alternative political ideas as political events, in co-opting, incorporating and subsuming any radical alternatives.

The 'mirror-like' nature of liberal egalitarianism allowed for a kind of reflection or translation of Marxist, feminist and anti-colonial arguments into the language of liberal egalitarianism, 'domesticating' and thus stifling their original critiques. By a strange paradox of exclusion, these alternatives do not themselves get much space in Forrester's book. In telling the story of liberal egalitarianism, Forrester's narrative proceeds for the most part in its shadow, with little means for taking up those neglected alternatives that remain in the dark. This is to a large extent unavoidable – the book covers a remarkable range of sources and philosophical ideas as it is – and does not reflect a lack of interest in these alternatives, but it is unclear whether this exclusion demonstrates Forrester's main contention or simply re-enacts it. Rather, the book is a kind of preparatory work, a genealogy that ties together Rawls, his times and his legacy in a way that makes very clear the need for a post-Rawlsian political philosophy. This is one reason why Forrester characterises the project of historicising liberal egalitarianism as an attempt to imagine a time before Rawls so totally reconceived the language, scope and ambitions of Anglophone political philosophy, when 'it was less certain what political philosophy was and what it could do', so that we too might think anew about what political philosophy is, and what it might do.

The final question then, is what political philosophy might look like. For Forrester, the fundamental problem with liberal egalitarianism was not its abstractions or idealisations, but that these abstractions were systematically depoliticising: consensus replaces conflict, arguments take the place of struggle, and like philosophy, politics appears to be little more than a matter of giving and receiving reasons. This depoliticising was possible because of Rawls' choice, from the veil of ignorance up, to ignore the 'normative relevance of arguments about how inequalities came about and, with them, non-institutional claims about individual entitlements, initial endowments, and the ownership of resources'. Such an approach must repoliticise political philosophy: it is not enough to apply ready-made normative theories to 'public affairs', especially not theories grounded in the idealisations of a vanished age. Instead it would confront the messy, decidedly un-ideal relations of power and domination that shape the world as it presents itself to us today. A new political philosophy inspired by the formerly 'domesticated' alternatives would mean more than providing new answers to Rawls' questions. It would have to fundamentally reconceive of the relation between political philosophy and history, and between politics and philosophy itself, emerging from under the shadow of justice radicalised by its renewed contact with historical reality.

Jonathan Egid

Interwoven solidarities

Brenna Bhandar and Rafeef Ziadah, eds, *Revolutionary Feminisms: Conversations on Collective Action and Radical Thought* (London: Verso, 2020). 240 pp., £17.99 pb., 978 1 78873 776 0

In striving towards revolutionary feminisms against a backdrop of world-changing events, the need for collective solidarity has never been more important. Brenna Bhandar and Rafeef Ziadah's book begins with this striking statement of clarity, first in the powerful and careful introduction written by the editors, and then in a sensitive unpacking across conversations with Avtar Brah, Gail Lewis, Vron Ware, Himani Bannerji, Gary Kinsman, Leanne Betasamosake Simpson, Silvia Federici, Ruth Wilson Gilmore, Avery F. Gordon and Angela Y. Davis. This point is contextualised further by Bhandar and Ziadah on the opening page:

> The feminisms we explore in this book are rooted in various political contexts and situated within a variety of political traditions. In fact, they are too diverse to easily name under a single heading… All of the individuals interviewed here, along with ourselves, may not agree on every detail – but we share the belief that freedom

requires revolutionary transformations in the organisation of the economy, social relations, political structures, and psychic and symbolic worlds, and that this must take place across multiple scales – from intimate relations between individuals to those among individuals, communities and the state.

Setting the book up as a platform for this work, the ten conversations push beyond the limiting scope of small differences to engage revolutionary feminist frameworks across entangled, intergenerational evolutions of language and approach. The book brings feminist, black, brown, indigenous, queer, anti-racist, de-colonial and anti-capitalist resistance movements together, in interwoven threads of collective action and radical thought. *Revolutionary Feminisms* sites itself at this axis of collaboration, as the literal frame of the book enacts the necessary methodological framework of solidarity, which revolutionary feminisms cannot be without.

The 'Acknowledgements' section describes the completion of the book in March 2020, during the first COVID lockdown. The launch that October took place online, as the pandemic unfolded with disproportionate global effects. The palpable enthusiasm for the publication of *Revolutionary Feminisms* at this critical time supports the authors' intention: these conversations might be a catalyst for further discourse, thought and action, around its central themes. The necessity to move events online allowed for an (un)situating of the book's discourse in terms of the contexts it speaks of and to, both locally and internationally. Reading the book at the end of 2020 and the start of 2021, it became part of a toolkit of guidance and collective feminist support – a toolkit all the more necessary in the solitary confines of lockdown, contending with the global events that Lisa Lowe points to in her sharp analysis in the 'Afterword'. The years of research, development and writing that produced these conversations emerged at a particular time of unravelling, and aim to attend and support a continuum of 'unfinished activisms' that are ever more acutely necessary.

The collection of conversations is devised around a cluster of central subjects, starting with Avtar Brah, Gail Lewis and Vron Ware's discussions of Diaspora/ Migration/ Empire. The evolution of Avtar Brah's work on the terms of diaspora-as-method comes through lived experience and the influence of radical women's resistance movements, seen for example in her work with the Southall Black Sisters from 1979 onwards. Drawing on Paul Gilroy's terms of *route* and *rootedness*, Brah explains how if diaspora can be understood through its 'connected spaces of knowledge and power', it can be utilised as an investigative process into the constituting conditions and contexts of its making. Through this unpacking, Brah re-introduces the concept of *belonging* – as the opposite of exclusion – and the further need for expanded community frameworks.

Touching also on the complexity of belonging, Gail Lewis describes how this notion is often precariously situated through a set of limiting parameters. Underlining the importance of lived experience in engaging questions of race, Lewis positions the personal as political, particularly when observed and positioned through the scale of the domestic. Lewis demonstrates the potential movement that can stem from this scale, building towards collective action and processes of political change. Lewis asserts the need to understand the 'presentness' of colonialism and empire; the erasure and 'disauthorising' of experiential violence it forces to take place. In turn the subjective and the 'felt' experience becomes a critique of the fallible frame of objective knowledge production. Gathering diverse knowledges becomes a way to challenge colonialism's ongoing, affective, asymmetric power structures.

Through a gendered reading of colonial history, Vron Ware discusses the development of her work on whiteness as a relational category that operates at the intersection of race, gender and class. A problematic absence of discourse on historical processes that produce whiteness allows the subject of race and racism to remain a predominantly non-white issue. Foregrounding a colonial 'presentness' in the construct of this condition, Ware frames this structural violence as something that takes place through a lack of responsibility or accountability, and points to intergenerational discourse as a pedagogical tool for dismantling racial violence, going beyond the scope of decolonisation to effect political change.

This initial collection of conversations reveals the interwoven nature of these discourses and their effects, as each describes the development of theory and practice through diasporic and migratory terms. They make it obvious that the figure of Empire cannot be escaped. In pointing to a 'deficit of historical thinking' in the discussed frameworks, we observe neo-colonial or 'neo-imperial' processes still at work – not a result of amnesia, but a product of the careful narrating of certain histories of exclusion. Each of these thinkers demands of us: how can diasporic and inter-generational methods work towards dismantling and rebuilding a better alternative?

In the section following, Himani Bannerji, Gary Kinsman, Leanne Betasamosake Simpson and Silvia Federici's conversations are framed through the subject of Colonialism/Capitalism/Resistance. Bannerji points to how nationalism produced a distorted independence in India, arguing that neo-colonial strategies have produced hierarchies of 'dependent capitalism', which uphold a corrupt class system. There is a need, therefore, for solidarity and strength to be found and shared across the experience of 'capitalist colonisation' towards true independence. Bannerji proposes that legal and social technologies and thresholds produced through a colonial hegemony must also be recognised. She analyses Crenshaw's argument for intersectionality, which, in the legal context of its development, is presented as a powerful tool for assigning legal accountability for race- and gender-based violence, along with its usefulness in describing and engaging discourse on complex intersections of this violence. Bannerji outlines how intersectionality seeks to hold the state accountable through legal mechanisms, despite the limitations of the law's foundational inequalities.

Both Bannerji and Kinsman connect through this point, as well as Frantz Fanon's writing, as Kinsman foregrounds Fanon's argument that Marxism needs to be 'stretched' to include and understand the lived experience of colonised and racialised people. Taking this further, Kinsman makes the argument for a queering of Marxism as a queering of the family and state.

Silvia Federici also points to Marxist roots in the formation of her political and intellectual feminist response to the violence of war, and the recognition of its fascistic and misogynist practices. Outlining the domestic space as an important site of political engagement and action, Federici points to the Wages for Housework campaign, which took the domestic space as a specific site of feminist struggle. This work critiqued forms of capitalist development that produced the domestic space as the location for unseen labour and neoliberalisms.

In contrast to discussions across the book on the neoliberalisation of education, in engaging Nishnaabeg intellectual practices, Leanne Betasamosake Simpson points to the ways that education and knowledge production also take place beyond institutions, within families and communities. She identifies the collective care of children as central to feminist, anti-colonial, anti-capitalist struggle, and the centrality of active, intergenerational participation in fomenting revolutionary change. Simpson takes the questions of solidarity forward as a condition of responsibility, predicated on 'relationships of care', arguing that generating alternative futures must be based on a deep understanding of relationality and the potential of a 'grounded freedom' in solidarity and self-determination. For indigenous peoples, this means not only critiquing and dismantling violence, but organising, reconstructing and struggling as a 'generative refusal', as a way of creating alternatives, even with the risk of failure.

We observe in these conversations the description and analysis of lived conditions born through colonialism and capitalism, forcing a spectrum of methods and practices of resistance in response. The points of contact that create these practices of resistance are often initiated from a specific entry point across intersectional subjects. It is in the acceptance of this certain failure, as fruitful recognition, that transformation and development allows these movements to become more holistically engaged.

In the last section of the book, Ruth Wilson Gilmore,

Avery F. Gordon and Angela Y. Davis discuss the subject of abolition feminism. Gilmore draws on her experience of growing up in a family of organisers and activists, which provided a foundation for her work on race, class and futures of Black radicalism. She discusses the development of her interdisciplinary methods in the field of geography. She describes how coming to the discipline with a background in radical Black thought shaped her approach, and how through this engagement she came to irrevocably change the field. Gilmore suggests that prison abolition is a specific form of anti-capitalism, a form specifically against racial capitalism. Gilmore foregrounds an important discourse on scale – from the body to the domestic to the global – from multi-scalar to inter-scalar relations of social reproduction, that engage political consciousness beyond lived experience. Revolutionary feminism requires understanding violence across these different scales, in order to understand its interconnectedness and effects.

Building on this insight, Gordon argues for a radical rethinking of the known forms of dispossession as a way of eliminating its violences. Outlining the spectre of 'haunting' as the presence of suppressed or concealed violent systems in the everyday, Gordon contends that we need to stop believing that the forces producing such violence are able to deter or end it. Without a full understanding of the complex histories of violence that produced the prison system, resistance movements will struggle to grasp what is involved in fighting the police and military. Gordon brings the role of the artist forward, especially in their potential for engaging the praxis of revolutionary feminist methods, a proposal that emerges in several places throughout the book.

In discussing the 'prison industrial complex' Davis exposes capital punishment as a racialised reflection of the violence of slavery in the present legal system. Davis argues that reform – whether of prisons, police or armed forces – cannot address the structural reasons for racist and repressive forms of punishment and security, at any scale of effect. In consequence, abolitionist theories and practices must engage with revolutionary approaches in the move towards justice and real social change.

Such a brief overview cannot do justice to the richness of each of these conversations. The collective insight that emerges across the volume serves as a powerful introduction to the foundational, intergenerational work undertaken across diverse and complex sites of feminist struggle. The conversational format draws on the vast wealth of knowledge, experience and scope of the interlocutors, giving personal insights into the evolution of these foundational feminist movements of collective resistance and radical thought. The book's framework serves to deepen our engagement with the work of revolutionary feminism, not as theory but as method and practice, fought and lived. As such, *Revolutionary Feminisms* is a tool of support for those currently engaged in ongoing feminist movements and struggles.

Several questions posed by Bhandar and Ziadah appear repeatedly, threaded across the different subjects. One example is the crucial question of the growing neoliberalisation of the systems of higher education. Perhaps connected to this is the question brought forward in the introduction in regards to Marx: the role of historical materialism. Articulated across the conversations is the necessary 'stretching' and 'building upon' of this work, as revolutionary feminist, anti-racist and decolonial thinkers challenge and rethink existing philosophical frameworks. The history of feminist work which this books charts shows that – whilst this may feel difficult and unprecedented – it has been an on-going process of change, both incremental and monumental.

Now into the second year of the COVID pandemic, with no real, sustainable, global end in sight, I continue to draw on the arguments made in this book for my own understanding of a complex, interlinked condition – the violence of patriarchy, colonialism, empire, racism, capitalism and ableism. The undoing of these interconnected structures of violence needs a careful and sensitive understanding of this complexity, the *longue durée* of this lived and built condition. 'Revolutionary feminisms' are not a theoretical framework, but are made and unmade through lived experience, struggle and political consciousness. There has never been a more important time to take heed of the message in this publication, delivered through a chorus of powerful voices: revolutionary feminisms need to become a revolution of solidarity.

Helene Kazan

'on the roots of olive trees uprooted'

Joseph Pugliese, *Biopolitics of the More-Than-Human: Forensic Ecologies of Violence* (Durham: Duke University Press, 2020). 312pp., £87.00 hb., £21.99 pb., 978 1 47800 767 8 hb., 978 1 47800 802 6 pb.

In 2001 the United Nations enacted an International Day for Preventing the Exploitation of the Environment in War and Armed Conflict (it's on 6 November, 12 days before World Philosophy Day). It is an honourable, if misguided gesture that at least points to the ways that armies and states deliberately or indiscriminately target people, their homes and infrastructures through acts of violence. Many of these forms of violence are done 'outside' of war, from nuclear testing areas of the western USA, and south Pacific islands, to the polluted soils, and waters around military bases in Alaska, Siberia, Diego Garcia, and beyond. Armies are exempted from even the barest, inadequate legislative restrictions on pollutions that nation states enact. And as many geographers have made clear, what the military has done to landscapes has been complemented by their work on what is known of landscapes – mapping, surveying, bordering the terrain.

Joseph Pugliesi focuses on this military destruction of more-than-human life, the soils, waters, airs, animals and plants and the legal aspects of such destructions, arguing that non-humans are just as much targeted and affected by military and state violence. He then makes the increasingly vocalised point that 'the environment' is covered in only a patchwork way by international law and despite calls for a fifth Geneva convention or convention on ecocide (something Extinction Rebellion amongst other groups have begun to support), destruction can be, and is, undertaken with impunity.

In recent years forensic architecture – the production and presentation of architectural evidence, relating to failed or destroyed buildings, urban conflict, within legal and political processes – has been developed to try to counter human rights violations, environmental destructions and extra-judicial killings. In this book Pugliese focuses on what he terms forensic ecologies, that relate to the ways forensics has been taken up as a 'field of action' in social sciences to detect and confront state violations – as the collection *Forensis* (2014) puts it.

Forensic anthropology predates other disciplinary take ups, and has been closely linked to crimes and war victims, whilst forensic media has pointed to the ways that audiovisual media technologies help reconstructions of events by accident investigators. The latter approaches are increasingly part of forensic architecture's practice too. Forensic auditing or accounting is increasingly used to detect crimes. Environmental forensics, as an approach, was invoked by Paulo Tavares' writings about the notorious Chevron pollution case in the Ecuadorian Amazon that resulted in a still unpaid $18 billion fine in 2011. Here, 'interrogating the earth' for crimes committed made us realise that such forensics have been central to environmental legal struggles for a long time. Pugliese's forensic ecologies is most similar to the latter:

> I deploy the concept to examine physical remains, in particular, of more-than-human entities left in the aftermath of the violence and destruction unleashed in zones of militarised occupation. I treat these remains as though they were evidence of culpable war crimes that must be brought to justice, even though currently they are necessarily proscribed by law.

In her recent essay 'Violence' Shela Sheikh has argued: 'To think violence today requires that we reposition ourselves, philosophically, legally, politically and ethically, in the space between certain extremes, themselves built upon violent historical categorisations and exclusions: human/nonhuman, subject/object, culture/nature, physis/tekhnē, active/passive.' It is in this between space that Pugliesi seems to situate his work. His examples are drawn from the actions of the Israeli state, U.S. military and Palestinian peoples.

At the core of this book are discussions around witnessing; not just of the destructions of people's homes and bodies or the ways crossing points forced on Palestinians are comparable to the ways animals are treated as they are moved towards slaughter houses. These are witnessed here, but what are also witnessed are the ways bodies of animals, trees, soils are woven into every aspect of peopled life, and how these relationships of everyday landscapes are being destroyed. This witnessing then is of a virtual kind, and it is of the degraded bodies of the violence of occupation of which forensic ecologies are made.

Pugliesi argues that his version of forensics differs from more legal forms. This is also where the relational materialism that is evident in much of the theorising in the introduction addresses criticisms made of the latter by indigenous scholars who accuse it of failing to acknowledge the ontologies and political practices that many new materialisms appear to echo. For Pugliesi, indigenous understandings of sciences entail being open to the roles of sensation, perceptions, affects, aspects usually shut out of western scientific discourses. He argues that in their practices forensic scientists are taught to listen to the way things speak in the trace evidences of a crime scene, a kind of animist vision of the world that is then, one gets the impression, stripped out when converted into formal evidence, with soils, plants, and other things reduced to mere background. If we are to follow this view of forensic science, making a strong distinction between 'indigenous' knowledges and 'western' sciences appears to make little sense, with indigenous groups using varied knowledges, ones which work for their situations, including sciences. Pugliese proposes a distinct definition of forensics that keeps in play ecological sites and actors:

> *Forensic evidence*, as I deploy the term, is constituted by a narrator, spatiotemporal markers, affective and rhetorical elements, and the complex interplay between an ecological site and the material actors that enable an entity to assume its veridictional status.

Most discussions of violence in subsequent chapters take their lead from a narrator, an eyewitness or documented account published by other authors which are then reiterated through various theoretical concatenations. So, in the middle section of the book Pugliese introduces us to a raft of what he terms biopolitical modalities: pedonpolitics, aeropolitics, aquapolitics, phytopolitics, zoopolitics – in this case to describe the predatory actions of the Israeli military state 'that require the state to exercise different techniques of operation in order to realise its intended bio-or necropolitical goals … These different modalities of statist operation are tributaries that flow from the governing category of biopolitics'. When discussing phytopolitics he invokes the work of Carol Bardenstein on how Israeli National Parks, picnic areas and camping grounds have been developed on the lands of some of the many hundreds of destroyed Palestinian villages. She documents a visit with refugee ex-residents to one destroyed village in Galilee that reveals a 'layer of memory' under the trees planted by the Jewish National Fund, of rubble from homes, but also of plants – pomegranates, fig trees, palms and lemon that have 'survived the JNF's erasure of the Palestinian village'. Pugliese runs with this example into a 'phytosemiotics of biocultural history' – the attentiveness of the refugees to what the trees 'have to tell them'. In this section we hear also of the water expropriation by settlers and state that makes some land increasingly impossible to cultivate. Land defined by the state as 'dry, barren' can then be claimed by the state. Elsewhere, Irus Braverman has also looked at the making of National Parks as 'green grabbing' around East Jerusalem, which, in effect, annexes land without compensation.

As we are so often reminded, land is the ultimate goal of settler colonialism, and imposed, deviously devised property relations the primary means of realising it. Yet land comprises water, soil, trees, so Pugliesi also takes us through examples of the poisoning of Palestinian water sources through deliberate sewage pollution by settlers, the ways that Palestinian plants, trees and farm animals are deliberate targets of the military and settlers, and more, through his explications of biopolitical modalities. This leads to much twisting and turning around autoimmunity discourses on how self-destruction results from supposed self-protection in the ways that these biopolitical modalities of aquapolitics, zoopolitics, and more, increasingly come to detrimentally affect the settler colonialists themselves and not just Palestinians.

This layering or reiterating of others' documented events through theory is an approach that mostly works, though it can take a little getting used to. Pugliese can bring theories together to make deeper points well, but it can sometimes fall flat, as in a story originally documented by Nadera Shalhoub-Kevorkian of a Palestinian family violently evicted from their house to make way for settlers and their child's recollections of the lemon tree of their garden. What it gains through being reiterated via theoretical tropes is debatable.

The value of this book is in bringing the relations of the human and nonhuman together to show that Israeli, U.S. or indeed any military colonial systems of control operate not just through the bodies of people, but also

the bodies of animals, soils, air, waters. Resistances can work through these bodies too, a point Zoe Todd has also made. Resistance to colonial dispossession is articulated and mobilised not only through human means, but also through the bones and bodies of animals, and we might add the roots, fruits and leaves of trees, soils, water bodies, and more. As such, these become aspects of a continually made and re-made more-than-human terrain. But it is sometimes hard to see this resistance as very effective rather than affective, especially when Pugliese points to the ways Israeli weapons and security firms can market new weapons and technologies as having been field tested on live populations – a very ugly sense in which bodies are targeted for knowledge, power, money, and because those bodies are seen as lesser. Many of those arms companies in Israel are partners now with EU border security agencies like Frontex, engaging in the highly profitable war on migrants as well.

Other witnessings and justifications recounted by Pugliese include a reading of official reports, letters and accounts on the imprisonment of Guantanamo prisoners Adnan Latif, Ahmed Errachidi and Mansoor Adayfi, and the ways they seemed to draw sustenance from ants, birds, banana rats, iguanas, and other creatures that could move across, in and out of the boundaries of the cages, prison and even maximum isolation cells. For Pugliese, through intimate contact such as soliciting for food, such animals create 'the Open'. In this space they give hope to men who have been swept up in operations by the U.S. military that finds it is all but impossible to countenance that such men are people. It is again a slowly powerful and distressing read. A final chapter deals with forensic ecologies of drone death, a recounting of witness statements of the after effects of the outrageous and unforgivable USA drone attacks on Yemeni villages. Airwars recently estimated that between 22-48,000 civilians have been killed by the USA since 2001 through more than 91,000 drone and airstrikes across mainly Islamic countries.

At the core of forensics in its different forms is some

notion of justice. Pugliese seeks to argue for justice for non-humans inevitably caught up or deliberately targeted in military and para-military violence. To do this he seeks to draw on various indigenous philosophies that offer an expanded non-anthropocentric sense of justice focused on 'all our relations' along with the concept of ecological justice. Here he invokes forms of earth jurisprudence that he argues are ascendent and that seemingly point a way to ecocentric law – that of Ecuador's constitutional rights of nature, Bolivia's Rights of Mother Earth / Pachamama framed in the constitution by Evo Morales' government, and the legal recognition of Te Urewera Park in New Zealand with its own 'legal personhood'. Such revisions to law are seen to extend legal systems and ethical obligations to the 'outlaws' of trees, soils, animals and mountains, with legal categories emanating from relationships rather than species. Pugliese makes a lot of claims for these approaches, particularly around how they question property relations, but these discussions, though interesting, feel underdeveloped here. If mainstream environmental laws have been about regulating the use of the earth through property relations, and are therefore human activity-centred, then law is indeed an area where fundamental transformations in living need to be made, moving towards something more earth-centred. We need more discussions of how this can work when extended outside of indigenous groups that tend to initiate or inspire such earth-centred laws, but also a sense of realism that earth jurisprudence is only complimentary to political struggle.

This review's title is taken from Iman Annab's poem 'An Ode to a Palestinian Olympian Living Under Occupation' (2016)

Chris Wilbert

Protests against reality

John Molyneux, *The Dialectics of Art* (Chicago: Haymarket Books, 2020). 300pp., £17.99 pb., 978 1 64259 131 6

This book is a significant contribution to the Marxist reflection on art. This is not a 'Marxist history of art', but a Marxist book about art, composed of various essays, some of a general theoretical character, and others concrete studies of artists. It has the great advantage of avoiding the most frequent shortcomings of Marxist works in this area: the fetishisation of 'realism', leading to the rejection of 'non-realist' art; the mechanical economic reductionism; the explanation of art as a pure 'reflection' of existing social conditions; the exclusive interpretation of art works as the expression of 'class ideologies'.

How to define art? Ernst Gombrich tried to avoid the difficulty by simply explaining that 'art is what artists do'. Fine, but how do you define an artist? Gombrich's explanation is both circular and empty. Molyneux's proposal is: art is one of the forms of *non-alienated labour*, a 'free' labour whose works are characterised by the *unity of form and content*. This is a quite persuasive proposition, although it depends on the meaning of 'form' …

Marx believed that 'capitalist production is hostile to art and poetry'. This provides, according to Molyneux, an objective basis for the alliance between the Left and Art. Of course, some artists were reactionary – Italian futurists, Ezra Pound, to mention only a few – but most, in the last 200 years, have been left-leaning, from Gustave Courbet to Banksy.

How is one to judge art? The criteria most used in the Western tradition, by art historians, critics and artists themselves, have been: mimesis, skill, beauty, the sublime, morality, emotional power, realism, originality, critical force. Molyneux does not reject these criteria, but tries to show their limits. For instance, 'realism', which after Marx and Engels, was picked up by wide sections of the Left as *the* criterion cannot be seen as the only one, simply because this excludes too much great art, from Leonardo da Vinci to Pablo Picasso.

In a chapter discussing the dialectics of modernism, Molyneux quotes an argument by Trotsky: creative art always begins with a protest against reality, either conscious or unconscious, active or passive, optimistic or pessimistic; with official academic recognition, the rebellion is neutralised. However, soon afterwards, a fresh revolt emerges, with a new generation: 'Through these stages passed classicism, romanticism, realism, naturalism, symbolism, impressionism, cubism, futurism'. Discussing the evolution of contemporary art from a similar perspective, Molyneux argues that, with the transformation of much contemporary art into the preserve of the super-rich, and the complicity of artists in this process, a 'fresh revolt' appeared, in the form of a *social turn* in modernism: the attempt at a socially-engaged art, moving out of the galleries, and joining protests, rallies and strikes.

Most of the book is dedicated not to general theoretical arguments, but to studies of specific artists, from Michelangelo to Picasso, Rembrandt to Emin. I'm afraid I cannot share Molyneux's interest, even enthusiasm, for some contemporary artists such as Emin and Damien Hirst (in his early works). And I'm a bit surprised that he makes only cursory references to surrealism, by far the most revolutionary movement in modern art. Some surrealist artists, such as Max Ernst or Joan Miro, are favourably mentioned, but others are summarily dismissed. This is the case with Salvador Dalí, 'certainly the most famous surrealist, but his art', Molyneux writes, 'despite its mimetic surface facility, within fairly naturalist representation (of "surrealistic" fantasy scenes), says little or nothing of power or insight about mid-twentieth-century social relations. Essentially, it is superficial sensationalism'. I disagree. During his first years – before becoming, as Breton said, 'Avida Dollars' – Salvador Dalí produced some extraordinary paintings, which belong to the most impressive documents of the surrealist imagination. He was also the co-author, with Luis Buñuel, of the picture *L'Age d'Or* (1930), a radically subversive film, a burning protest against all prevailing social relations, which was outlawed, as a danger to public order, for 50 years by the French authorities. If there is a modern artist to whom the qualification of 'naturalist sensationalism' applies, it is not Dalí, but Damien Hirst.

Nevertheless, Molyneux has a beautiful chapter on Rembrandt, discussing his relation to the Dutch revolution of the seventeenth century and to bourgeois individualism: his self-portraits are one of the wonders of world culture in their visual representation of the individual 'soul'. Moreover, his humanist viewpoint and his empathy with the outcasts and outsiders of Dutch society – gypsies, beggars, Jews – clash with bourgeois values.

The best chapter of the book is, I believe, on 'Michelangelo and Human Emancipation'. It is an outstanding essay, a brilliant excursion in Marxist art history, with few equivalents. Michelangelo belongs to the very small band of individuals – Aristotle, Shakespeare, Goethe, Mozart – who seem to tower over history. How to explain this exalted standing, at the summit of human achievement? Ancient art historians, such as Vasari, refer to his 'divine inspiration'. A secular version of this argument can be found in Gombrich: Michelangelo is a genius, and 'genius cannot be explained'. Trying to provide a more substantial argument, critics, from Vasari to Gombrich, refer to Michelangelo's mimetic skill, the astonishing realism of his paintings. Molyneux rightly criticises this interpretation: was Michelangelo really 'immitating' nature or 'representing reality'? In fact, his art is not at all naturalistic: a work like the Sistine Chapel fresco, *The Creation of Adam*, is very far from any 'reality'. To understand the meaning of his art, it is necessary to refer to its historical context. The Italian Renaissance, an early stage in the rise of European capitalism, was a huge step forward in the emancipation of the human personality. As Engels emphasised, 'Renaissance man' had a fullness of character, which was lost with the servitude of the capitalist division of labour. Michelangelo's art, in works like the David sculpture in Florence or *The Creation of Adam* at the Vatican, express this more clearly, more powerfully and more beautifully than perhaps any other artist in European history. Of course, there is no mechanical relation between his art and the social and economic conditions of his time, as, for example, the Althusserian art historian Nicos Hadjinicolau seemed to believe; the artist actively responds to deep social forces by developing a personal vision, based on his unique experience. This is an experience which includes, for Michelangelo, a strong homoerotic component, obvious in his paintings, but generally ignored by art historians.

Discussing the Sistine Chapel frescos, Molyneux contrasts the humanist optimism of the ceiling, *The Creation of Adam*, with the pessimism and anguish of the wall: *The Last Judgement*. As Arnold Hauser pointed out, this last piece is 'a picture of bewilderment and despair, no longer "beautiful"'. How to explain the tragic atmosphere of this painting, and of all of Michelangelo's artworks that follow? What happened between the ceiling (1508-12) and the wall (1535-41)? In 1533 the Medicis returned to power, bringing an end to the Republic of Florence, which had the active sympathies of Michelangelo, and inaugurating 200 years of hereditary Medici rule. That was the end of the Renaissance dream of human liberty in Florence. Although Michelangelo depended on commissions from the Medicis and the Pope for his work, he was often in conflict with them.

Among Michelangelo's late works figure the mysterious 'slaves' sculptures, considered by many art historians to be 'unfinished'. Molyneux believes that the artist, in conscious or unconscious ways, created four gigantic figures struggling for freedom from the stone, but still held captive by it: a powerful statement about human history and the struggle for human emancipation as a whole. Are we not today, five hundred years later, still fighting for freedom, still gripped by the rock of class society?

Michael Löwy

Throwing rocks

Avery F. Gordon, *The Hawthorn Archive: Letters from the Utopian Margins* (New York: Fordham University Press, 2018). 472pp., £87.00 hb., £33.00 pb., 978 0 82327 631 8 hb., 978 0 82327 632 5 pb.

In discussing with Avery F. Gordon his video installation, *The Beginning. Living Figures Dying* (2013), a project focused 'on the relationship between actors and sculpture in film', the German artist Clemens von Wedemeyer tells of the myth of Deucalion and his wife Pyrrha and their survival from the wrath of Zeus. Upon hearing the myth Avery F. Gordon concludes: 'at the end, we return to the beginning, to a story about the origin of human life from stone, and to what, at this point in our history, we are capable of believing in.' In order to understand why Gordon reaches such a conclusion upon hearing this myth it is pertinent to turn to the myth itself.

Deucalion and Pyrrha were the only survivors of the flood that the capricious Zeus instigated for no reason other than his wish to punish humanity. The myth originally narrated by Ovid in Book I of the *Metamorphoses* talks of these two survivors' loneliness, their desire to renew humanity and their unique interpretation of the Oracle of Themis, which advised them 'to veil their heads and cast their great mother's bones behind them if they wanted to renew humanity'. Deucalion and Pyrrha decided it would be hubristic to throw their mother's bones backwards so instead they cast stones, thereby creatively interpreting the reference to their mother's bones as corresponding to mother earth and stones respectively. Deucalion's stones gave birth to men, Pyrrha's to women. The myth reminds us, as Gordon points out, that humanity is inextricably linked to earth, and that it is in our hands to acknowledge this connection, to ensure that we don't drive ourselves to extinction by encouraging ecological catastrophe.

This archive is just one example of the myriad materials – letters, photographs, art, recipes – that Gordon interpretively gives us in *The Hawthorn Archive*, and it epitomises its contents. As Gordon informs us, *The Hawthorn Archive* borrows its name 'from the forest tree' Hawthorn which is 'known for its longevity' and 'favoured by witches and those internationalists who celebrate the first of May'. The rationale for having the name of a tree heading the book is not made explicit by Gordon. We can only speculate that the longevity of the tree, and its being favoured by radicals, gives rise to hope for an enduring and radical archive.

Whilst Gordon is a sociologist by training, this book diverts from standard sociological writings about utopia, which often either study *existing* utopian communities or offer methodological advice on how to engage with the concept of utopia. Instead, Gordon offers an innovative practice-based approach, to *create* a utopian archive out of the unrealised dreams of those who struggled and are still struggling for freedom and equality. Indeed, like Deucalion and Pyrrha who recreated the world by throwing a stone backwards, Gordon (re)creates a new way of seeing utopia. She throws a stone at traditional understandings of utopia received from Thomas More, Ernst Bloch, Ursula Le Guin and others, not as an act of violence but as an act of creation, creating anew a vision of utopia as 'a collective life without misery, deadly inequalities, mutating racisms, social abandonment, endless war, police power, authoritarian governance, heteronormative impositions, patriarchical rule, cultural conformity and ecological destruction'.

Utopia, from the Greek, was introduced into English by Thomas More in 1516, and, as is well-known, literally means non-place. Utopia, More tells us, is an island located in the New World, which was discovered by Raphael Nonsenso, a companion of Americo Vespucci. The island features an egalitarian political system, where its inhabitants benefit from the lack of private property, universal health care and free education. Since More, utopia has been painted in leftist colours and imagined as a desirable radical project with a future orientation. More's island utopia is made up of 'fifty four splendid big towns ... all with the same language, laws, customs, and institutions', designed the same and adorned with indistinguishable buildings. More's *Utopia* features what may initially seem like desirable characteristics. But the more we reflect on the novel, the more we notice that the island of utopia does not involve such an egalitarian society after all. In *Utopia*, slaves and women are not equal to free men. This good place is revealed to be, as Le Guin perceived, Euclidean, Eurocentric, masculinist and imperialist. Gordon notes that our utopian imaginings, primarily influenced by More and other European writers, are exclusionary and sets out on a journey to unearth and build an inclusive archive, bringing to the surface the creativity, thinking, practices and sacrifices made by people such as the Black American worker Harry Haywood (counterposed to William Morris), the philosophy of happiness of C.L.R. James (counterposed to Ernst Bloch) and the Combahee River Collective (counterposed to the separatist middle-class community Brooke Farm).

The Hawthorn Archive is divided into four parts 'promoting and keeping safe the subjugated knowledges of the nobodies'. Section I explains how the archive is being produced – that it existed prior to Gordon and her collaborators bringing it together – its collaborative character (it uses extensive correspondences, art work and any other materials that her collaborators deposited) and offers a critique of Eurocentric understandings of utopia that draw on the work of Toni Cade Bandara. The means and methods (running away, deserting) used to create a better life are introduced through the writings of Cederic J. Robinson. Eliza Winston the Black American slave who earned her freedom by running away, deserting soldiers and others are presented in Section II. Section III offers rich insights into the labour, trauma and stress that it takes to build freer and more egalitarian societies. In this section Gordon considers the subjectivity of utopians and what it takes to challenge, attack and dismantle institutions of power and domination. In Section IV the thoughts of curator Anslem Franke regarding the nature of time haunt Gordon. Time, he tells us is not linear – past, present, future – but rather scrambled. As he explains, '[t]he future is now behind us, and the past approaches us from the front.' Haunted by his observations Gordon goes on to search for those dreams, writings, and thoughts that have *not yet* been realised. In doing so, she presents us with an archive of unrealised dreams drawn from the reflections of those that engaged or had been with prisoners (i.e., Emma Goldman, Rosa Luxemburg), archive and films about workhouses (i.e., Breitenau) or files regarding prison war camps (i.e., Halfmoon Prison war camp).

The textual (i.e., letters, writings, recipes) and visual (i.e., photographs, drawings, film stills) archive deposited and curated by Gordon and collaborators brings to life the subjugated knowledges of 'slaves, indentured servants and maids, prisoners, conscripts, pirates, sailors, religious heretics, woodcutters, water carriers, prostitutes, indigenous peoples, commoners, runaways, deserters and vagabonds', and so creates an alternative utopian imaginary, one that does not paint the road to freedom and equality (economic, political, social) with rosy colours. Her protagonists paved the way to our freer world (albeit one that still needs major structural transformations) by sacrificing or endangering themselves. Utopian worlds, Gordon concludes, are not worlds located in the future. On the contrary, they exist in the very crux of our present and are made by those who we fail to notice, acknowledge or recognise as utopian. Utopia is not built overnight, nor is it build in isolation, without the collaboration of others. Individualism and no possible exit from the alienating current conditions is the myth propagated by utopia's not-so-friendly sibling, dystopia, a myth that Gordon elegantly undoes, showing that a better world is possible.

The rich content of *The Hawthorn Archive* enables us to see the truth about utopia, its exclusions, the effort that it takes to build a fairer society. Nevertheless, whilst the content of Gordon's archive may displace More's definition of utopia, its form does not differ dramatically from the props and dramaturgy used in *Utopia*. Like More, Gordon uses epistolography to transmit the development of her and her collaborators' idea of utopia; like More she uses dialogue to convey ideas; and, like More, she uses images to convey location or different languages. *The Hawthorn Archive*, despite the radicality of its content, is rather conventional in form.

Additionally, whilst the book invokes numerous utopian voices, it leaves unresolved the tension between those utopians who think that the structure of the state (radical left legalists) can be the vehicle for a free and egalitarian society and those who see the state (i.e., anarchists) as the obstacle to a better life. The book may include a recipe for celery soup, but there is of course no simple recipe for resolving such a tension. The tension nevertheless holds the promise of utopia not being totalised or closed, a potential danger of utopia that Jorge Luis Borges warns about in 'A Weary Man's Utopia'. This tension is an invitation to continue the work of utopia, bring our own subjugated knowledges to *The Hawthorn Archive*, collaborate with it in perpetuity so as to keep dystopia at bay.

Elena Loizidou

Race after information-value

Seb Franklin, *The Digitally Disposed: Racial Capitalism and the Informatics of Value* (Minneapolis: Minnesota University Press, 2021). 254pp., £86.00 hb., £19.00 pb., 978 1 51790 714 3 hb., 978 1 51790 715 0 pb.

As our tech overlords flee a blighted planet, a scholarly consensus is taking shape around the fallout of unchecked innovation and the subsequent need for 'algorithmic justice'. This consensus is perhaps distilled by Shalini Kantayya's award-winning 2020 documentary *Coded Bias*, which tells the story of Joy Buolamwini, a researcher who, in the course of her work at the MIT Media Lab, uncovered a design flaw embedded in facial recognition systems: certain of these AI-driven technologies fail to accurately register dark-skinned faces. To supplement its retracing of Buolamwini's journey from this discovery to the floor of the U.S. House of Representatives, the film includes interviews with Cathy O'Neil, Virginia Eubanks, Zeynep Tüfekçi, Safiya Umoja Noble, Meredith Broussard and Shoshana Zuboff, thinkers who are among the torchbearers of a growing body of research on information technologies' role in entrenching and perpetuating inequalities of race, gender and class. Exploring how historical modes of subjugation live on in algorithms, surveillance technologies and other mobilisations of big data, such studies often conclude – much as *Coded Bias* does – with overtures to transparency, fairness and ethics, proposals for socially conscious approaches to technological design and use, and calls for increased governmental regulation of the industry.

But what if Buolamwini's discovery were no glitch at all? What if instead it were an index of an inherently *informatic* logic – not simply one underpinning contemporary techno-imaginaries, but one central to the racialising and gendering dynamics from which capitalism draws? These are among the questions that Seb Franklin's highly ambitious *The Digitally Disposed* indirectly poses and enables us to answer. Yet, while Franklin's text may be related in theme to the body of work mentioned above, its contributions lie in its dramatically different approach to the Gordian knot of information and inequality. For whereas the conversations animating Kantayya's film tend to foreground contemporary practices and products fuelled by data, *The Digitally Disposed* shifts our attention to an epistemological mode that historically connects the trans-Atlantic slave trade with the seemingly immaterial realm of digital computing.

It is this mode that Franklin terms the 'informatics of value', a formulation that signals how 'information' and 'value' constitute a homology that subtends the material pasts and presents of racial capitalism. This ultimately leads Franklin to rearticulate both parts of his work's subtitle as together representing 'a system of accumulation based on "spontaneous" interconnection, dispossession and differential integration'. Drawing on Black, Indigenous, postcolonial and feminist scholars, as well as on figures affiliated with the post-Marxist school of 'value-critique', Franklin's critical intervention lies in his demonstration of how the informatics of value as a mode of abstraction is acutely visible in (but necessarily precedes) much of the thought that laid the foundations of the Information Age. Through nuanced readings of the writings of cyberneticians and information theorists Claude E. Shannon, Norbert Wiener, Heinz von Foerster and R.S. Hunt, 'father of the computer' Charles Babbage and psychosociologist Jacob L. Moreno, as well as supplemental ones of literature and media by Elena Ferrante, Samuel Delany, Sondra Perry and Eduardo Williams, *The Digitally Disposed* implicitly calls not for a program of regulation and reform aimed at curbing bias in technological systems, but for the abolition of capitalism and value altogether.

Franklin begins by asking: How are the principal tenets of digital capitalism – e.g., that data transmission *is* commodity circulation and that freedom, self-expression and transmission capacity together constitute the key to flourishing – predicated on differentiation, connectivity and dispossession? Part I of the text, 'The Informatics of Value', offers readers the basis of a response in the form of a series of concepts that establish how the foundation of capitalist society, or 'value', has always been 'informatic'. These investigations extend Franklin's previous analyses in 2015's *Control: Digitality as Cultural Logic* – which centre on how 'digitality' 'posits its objects as already fundamentally discrete' and promises to render the world knowable through 'processes of capture, definition, optimisation and filtering' – by showing how that *cultural* logic is underwritten by a more general set of social relations (or 'forms of disposal') that, while specific to the longer history of racial capitalism, become most clearly legible at the dawn of the digital age.

These forms of disposal are shaped by capitalism's governing abstraction, the 'informatics of value'. A clearer vision of the concept is implicit, Franklin begins by explaining, in Gayatri Chakravorty Spivak's 'Can the Subaltern Speak?' and its recasting of capitalist value: instead of treating value as 'congealed quantities of homogeneous labour', Spivak asserts that 'under capitalism, *value*, as produced in necessary and surplus labour, is *computed* as the representation/sign of objectified labour'. Building on this framing, Franklin maintains that Marx's use of the word 'congealed' – or, the material process of boiling down animal matter to produce a jelly – does not fully capture the machinations of value, as, under this capitalism, bodies are affected in a way that not only marks and sorts them materially, but that also posits them as discrete nodes in a virtual network of exchange. This leads Franklin to note that while 'capital only recognises as valid that which is computed' (or that which can connect to what he terms the 'value network', itself a communicative refraction of the labour market), 'all labour entails some degree of *congelation*', or physical degradation. This is true – though to different degrees and ends – for the 'primitive accumulation' occasioned by the slave trade as it is for the precarity-inducing Uberisation of the present moment. Informed by thinkers such as Sylvia Wynter and Cedric Robinson (and indirectly calling to mind Caitlin Rosenthal's more recent analyses of slavery and quantitative management), here Franklin effectively prises the informatic from the more contemporary context of digitality to show how it epistemologically animates the entire history of racial capitalism. Reading an example from Olaudah Equiano's slave narrative, he registers that the enslaved body was mutilated during the Middle Passage before later being forced into bondage and worked often to death, and that the same body underwent a concomitant process of abstract objectification (or computation) wherein it became a discrete statistic that could be transmuted into value, the legible instantiation of which, on the auction block, would be its price.

On this basis, Franklin convincingly argues, this system of accumulation, insofar as it must reduce everything to discrete information/values, can be understood as one of 'differential computation' whose ascriptive and violent processes code race (as well as gender and ability) as difference. This central argument permits readers to grasp how Gregory Bateson's famous adage – that information is simply 'a difference that makes a difference' – is in fact a cypher for how the racialising movements of capital must together be seen as the 'value-informatic' computation of difference. Franklin in turn reasons that the informatics of value as the core abstraction of racial capitalism '*determines – or dominates – the concrete*'. In other words, the quasi-objective, impersonal social forms expressed by the categories of value and information do not simply disguise 'real' material social relations; rather, the abstract structures expressed by these categories *are* those 'real' social relations. Under racial capitalism, individuals *are* value as much as they *are* information.

Yet these arguments also highlight how value-informatic logic is not simply an ideological echo of some economic base, but rather a force that bends all of lived reality to its image. This material flip-side, Franklin suggests, can be glimpsed in the archives of computing, cybernetics, information science and sociometry. Across Part II, 'Media Histories of Disposal', Franklin turns to these sources to identify an idealised form of 'digital-liberal personhood' as well as specific binaries that ground the abstract domination of racial capitalism. These binaries, in making concrete the 'mirror world' of information-value, implicitly demand that we become 'reliable circuits' or face disposal – that we 'connect [to the value network] or die'.

These histories examine how such 'connection' depends on social relations – and not simply those of class – that differentially affect racialised and gendered populations. These forms may demand connection, but paradoxically require disconnection for their upkeep. Put otherwise, the worlds that these archives imagine are not new futures, but *digital* reformulations – and, in many ways, affirmations – of racial capitalism's differential computation of all into value. For example, Franklin shows how Wiener's techno-benevolence relies on a contrast between the optimal digital-liberal subject – understood as self-possessing, self-reproducing, upgradable and flexible – and 'mechanical slaves', a 'deplorable al-

ternative' (according to Wiener) defined by its 'foreclosed conditions of reproduction' and inability to secure 'wage-mediated access to the means of meeting basic needs'. The frictionless existence of digital-liberal personhood, in other words, is both counterposed to and made possible through the devaluation and dispossession of those deemed nonhuman.

This racialising penchant of value-informatic logic is elsewhere legible in Babbage's screed on 'intellectual workers' and 'street nuisances', Hunt's distinction between 'cleverness' and 'drive', and Moreno's social hierarchy of 'creators' and 'zootechnical animals'. In each case, the abstract, imagined ideal extracts the means of its existence from its opposite; form draws on formlessness, just as signal feeds on noise, just as the accumulation that Marx once described as 'primitive' is ongoing, propping up the very real illusions of digitality and capitalism, of information and value. 'This recognition', Franklin insists, entails 'the realisation that there is no spontaneous interconnection, no homeostatic reproduction; that computation cannot be separated from congelation; that the synthesis of reliable circuits requires the distribution of incapacity; and that it is necessary to find ways of living otherwise, modes of connection and relation not subordinated to the demand for accumulation'.

Such a call for the end of capitalism provides the grounds for a constructive reconsideration of certain more general links between technology and power, much as those brought to the fore by *Coded Bias*. Indeed, when considered through the lens of Franklin's arguments, the flaw discovered by Buolamwini in fact indexes the innerworkings of a system of accumulation that paradoxically depends on the differential computation of populations for its continued existence. Moreover, the demands for recognition, connection and transparency voiced by Kantayya's film and the scholarship of its interviewees are also eerily reminiscent of the abstract imaginaries that Franklin claims are determined by the informatics of value.

This problem of form determination also underpins certain of the text's methodological and theoretical contributions to literary and media studies. The first of these results from the fact that throughout his historical reconstitution of racial capitalism's core mode of abstraction, Franklin remains acutely aware of his investigation's limits. For while he ultimately concludes that it is the 'connections severed from the circulation of value' that constitute the 'foundations of the fullest collectivity', he resists the urge to prescriptively leverage his previous readings into political or aesthetic programs. By instead elevating thinkers whose work explicitly deals with collective forms and practices not predicated on information-value, *The Digitally Disposed* both encourages and lays out paths for similarly interdisciplinary research.

Finally, Franklin's insights about the abstract's domination of the concrete – particularly when thought alongside his close readings of novels, art installations and films – raise important questions about the very possibility of practices capable of existing outside of or counter to racial capitalism's forms of disposal. For example, if the logics that Franklin details are truly form-determining, what is the ontological status of artistic practice and its derivative objects? Can either function as anything but a reflection – however clarifying – of the informatics of value? By gesturing towards these and other issues, *The Digitally Disposed* establishes itself as critical reading and inspiration for the digital present, highlighting the continued need for anti-racist and anti-capitalist scholarship capable of rethinking the forms of knowledge and relation that connect our world.

Marc Kohlbry

Jean-Luc Nancy, 1940-2021
Joanna Hodge

> One day, what I am saying to you today will no longer have any sense or any handle on the period. But today this is where there is some sense: in saying sense is absent, in saying that this absence is what we are exposed to, and that this exposition constitutes what I will call not only our present history but, along with Rimbaud, our refound eternity.
>
> – Jean-Luc Nancy, 1993

With his recent death on 23 August 2021, Jean-Luc Nancy, the third of the Strasbourg thinkers, joins Jacques Derrida (1930-2004) and Philippe Lacoue-Labarthe (1940-2007) in the Elysian Fields of posthumous fame. The connections between these three are many and various, stretching from the early 1970s up until their deaths and beyond. In June 2004, Derrida attended one more conference at Strasbourg, organised in his honour, invoking town, university and department as his first and latest hosts. He wrote: 'I have just, no doubt in a rather abusive and unfaithful way, privileged, as I thought I had to, our trio.' (*For Strasbourg* 2014, 2004)* For Nancy, the importance of working and thinking with others provides a key to some otherwise puzzling features of his writing, his enthusiasm for the interview as a way of putting concepts in question, and his generous encouragement of those who sought to translate his writings.

In a conversation with Pierre-Philippe Jandin, published as *The Possibility of a World* (2017, 2013), he discusses his formative years and a sojourn from five to eleven years of age, at a school in Baden-Baden in post-war Germany, a child of a member of the French occupying forces. Nancy and Jandin discuss how his early student years and preparation for entry to the École normale supérieure ran in parallel with an exit from the Young Christian Movement and a separation from Roman Catholicism. He completed a doctorate in 1973 on Kant's analogies of experience, under the supervision of Paul Ricoeur, and was awarded a *doctorat d'état* in 1987 from the University of Toulouse for work subsequently published as *The Experience of Freedom* (1993, 1988). Jean-Francois Lyotard and Jacques Derrida were both on the examining committee, alongside the director of studies, Gerard Granel. In his conversation with Jandin, Nancy notes the impact on him of reading Derrida's study of Husserl, *Edmund Husserl's Origin of Geometry: An Introduction* (1978, 1962): 'As for me, the day that I discovered Derrida's text for the first time in 1964, a text that had been published in 1962, I felt that something was bursting open.' That text ends with Nancy expressing reservations concerning uses of Derrida's notion of a messianicity without messiah, to explore the surprise of what arrives, in defiance of expectation.

From 1973 Nancy taught for many years as Professor at the University of Strasbourg in conjunction with Philippe Lacoue-Labarthe, and, after retirement, remained attached as Emeritus Professor. He held at various times visiting professorships at Ohio State University, the University of California and the State University of New York. His ability to travel freely was seriously restricted following major surgery and a heart transplant in 1991, which was followed across the decades by complications following the requisite suppression of the auto-immune system, to prevent rejection of the organ. His anticipated lifespan was then a further ten years, which against the odds turned out to be nearly thirty years more life and activity. His condition is discussed by him with the film maker, Claire Denis, in her film *Vers Nancy* (2002), in which there emerges a shared commitment to an ontology of differences, and to assigning a priority to an analysis of acts, rather than of identities. He discusses the dismemberment of bodily integrity and a suspen-

---

* The dates here given for Nancy's writings are those of their English translation, followed by their original publication in French.

sion of any authoritative gaze, in relation to her highly controversial film, *Trouble Every Day* (2001). Here bodies are conceived and presented as collections of parts, blood smeared on surfaces, a *corpus* in fragments, *partes extra partes*, rather than as integrated *corps*, or unified organisms. A disintegration of bodies, and of sexual identities, in the grip of desire and sexual activity, returns for attention in the recently published conversations with Irving Goh, *The Deconstruction of Sex* (2021), for which there is no prior publication in French. Denis returns the compliment by responding to his essay on the transplant condition, in her film with the same name, *L'intrus* (2004). A concern for an immediacy of the cinematic image is even more salient in his extended study of the cinematography of Abbas Kiarostami, *The Evidence of Film* (2001).

Nancy's thinking is often associated with two provocative phrases: the 'inoperative community', which he explores in the wake of the writings and commitments of Georges Bataille and Maurice Blanchot, in proximity to those of Lacoue-Labarthe; and the 'deconstruction of Christianity', which he disputed with Derrida, who was sceptical about the implied privilege to Christianity. This deconstruction of Christianity is in turn associated in Nancy's enquiries with two further phrases, retained in Latin: firstly, from the Latin Mass, *hoc est enim corpus meum* (for this is my body), and *noli me tangere* (do not touch me), addressed by the risen Christ to Mary Magdalen, at the empty tomb on the Sunday morning of resurrection. These serve as disruptive pediments to Hegel's focus on a Good Friday of speculative dialectics. Each phrase captures a moment of substitution and metamorphosis. The first marks the transubstantiation of the communion wafer into the body of Christ, commemorating the sharing and divine revelation at the Last Supper, before the Crucifixion. The second marks the transitional status of that divine embodiment, in transit between human death and eternal, divine life. These phrases from the Christian tradition mark limit conditions within Christian doctrine and a disruption of boundaries between religious doctrine, on the one side, and, on the other, both metaphysical and artistic commitments and practices. For Nancy is committed to the thought that the arts and metaphysics of the Western world are irretrievably connected, in their development and dissolution, inventions and multiplication, to these moments of manifestation, in which presentation is conditional on an absence. For Nancy, the hospitality in Christianity to the making of images, and to a proliferation of narratives, marks it out from other monotheisms, Judaism and Islam, to which nevertheless Christianity in all its variants remains so intimately linked. He diagnoses this hospitality as one aspect of a tendency within Christianity to develop its own distinctive atheism and denial of divinity – in his phrase, an absentheism – and to a dissolution of a unified functioning religion.

Photograph: Daniele Silvestri (2008)

Two collections of papers, *Dis-enclosure: The Deconstruction of Christianity* (2008, 2005) and *Adoration: The Deconstruction of Christianity II* (2013, 2010) are preceded by a study of paintings of the encounter at the tomb between the risen Christ and Mary Magdalen, under the title, *Noli me tangere* (2008, 2004). There, delimitations and boundaries between day and night, the visible and the invisible, life and death, the human and the divine are traced across the apparently two-dimensional surface of a series of emblematic paintings. Here is another exploration of a truth in painting, *La vérité en peinture*, put in focus by Derrida in his study of 1978, affirming an inheritance of the technical and pedagogical functions of painting biblical scenes, in an age of general illiteracy. In *The Look of the Portrait* (2006, 2000), Nancy had already explored how the gaze of the one portrayed displays a world, not exposed as a spectacle in front of me, but rather as forces traversing a self, plunged into a world, and formed by those forces. In 'On the Threshold' (1993), a text read before Caravaggio's *The Death of the Virgin*, in the Louvre in 1992, Nancy writes: 'Here there is no message, and no passage. Between John and the two Marys, there is only a present of light, color, cloth and the body.' This connects to another key feature of his enquiries, a commitment to a version of materialism, itself in process of transformation, not held in place by given concepts, or an essence of matter, 'bound by no other essence than the inimitable existence of singularity.' The various materialities of art practice are to be respected in their distinctness.

Nancy affirms Heidegger's account of a withdrawal of being, leaving human beings in a world of inert entities, but proposes in addition an opening for an account of matter, as flows of forces forming singularities in an areality of the spaces those bodies occupy. In *The Experience of Freedom*, there is an invocation of a transcendental, or ontological materiality, as a site for the arrival of this areality, as a term for space, as occupied, extended and distended, by bodies. A primacy for a body in dispersal, *partes extra partes*, is subsequently expanded on, in writings collected under the title *Corpus* (2008, 1992), and developed in *Coming* (2017, 2014), in conversation with Adele van Reeth, and in *Sexistence* (2021, 2017), which explore the pleasure of sex and the interactive nature of a human experience of embodiment. These writings underpin Nancy's notion that there is something distinctive about human embodiment, but not to be defended on the basis of any imitation in the human of some divinely given form. He develops a commitment to modes of materialisation which occur across a boundary usually held in place between concepts of nature (*physis*) and concepts of artifice (*techne*). This generates an account of relations in the world as ecotechnics, systems of semio-technological transformation, most explicitly in *The Sense of the World* (1997, 1993) and in the essay in *Being Singular Plural* (2000, 1996), 'War, Right, Sovereignty-techne', where its status as successor term to political economy is rehearsed.

Being, sovereignty, divinity, are for Nancy all names for empty spaces, opening up as a consequence of a withdrawal of anachronised meanings and a decline of sclerotic institutions: spaces in which unprecedented and unconfigured forces gather and circulate, for good and ill. Christianity for Nancy is tied to a specific form of sovereign power, expressed in the papal phrase, *urbi et orbi*, addressing both city and globe, conjoining the city of Rome to a global reach. This global reach empties out any determinacy of meaning for its doctrinal commitments and generates an emergent distinction between weakening forces of world making, *mondialisation*, in which meanings are formed and contested, and expanding processes of globalisation, in which a single set of uniform relations, with systems of general equivalence, displaces and overrides localised systems of evaluation. In his pamphlet, *After Fukushima: The Equivalence of Catastrophes* (2014, 2012), responding to the earthquakes and nuclear disaster at Fukushima in 2011, Nancy meditates on the disruption of the boundary between natural and man-made disasters, and on the imminence of ecological catastrophe, both man-made and natural, across the globe. This provides the backdrop for his very recent discussion of the Covid pandemic in *Un trop humain virus* (2020), shortly to appear in English translation from Polity Press. There he deploys distinctions between three kinds of ill (*maladie, malheur, malfaisance*), illness, misfortune and ill-doing (malfeasance) as active harm-doing. A preoccupation with thinking evil is in evidence along the length of his enquiries. Already in *The Experience of Freedom*, he disputes Heidegger's seeming affirmation of Schelling on an ontodicy, a necessity for evil in the world, instead identifying evil-doing as hostility to, and the attempt to destroy, existence itself. It arrives again in a borrowing from Hannah Arendt, on a banality of evil, in *The Banality of Heidegger* (2017, 2015), his response to the anti-Semitic observations in Heidegger's commonplace books, recently published as the *Black Notebooks*. Thus the classically theological concept of evil is taken up and transposed, with the assistance of readings of Schelling, Nietzsche, Heidegger and Arendt, in a context no longer governed by theological concepts of good and evil, and the satanic and divine powers, which traditionally hold them in place. This move he also makes in relation to a concept of creation, in a fourth key text from the past twenty years: *The Creation of the World, or Globalisation* (2007, 2002), in which the phrase *urbi et orbi* is identified as marking an anonymised 'anywhere and everywhere'.

The theological notion of a creation of a single world as universe, out of nothingness, is there put into tension with human technological invention, resulting in multiple worlds. Nancy appropriates and redeploys Heideggerian themes – the end of philosophy as unified metaphysical system – and he develops a contrast between a single phenomenologically derived concept of a unified world, and multiple worlds, as lived in. Nancy champions a neglected articulation of *Mitsein*, a being with, in Heidegger's *Being and Time* (1962, 1927), as prior to and constitutive for an affirmation by Heidegger of a determinacy of being, *Dasein*, in its being-towards-death. He shares with Arendt a compensating emphasis on a moment of birth and on natality, as the arrival, and new entry into world making. Metaphysics, as a once-for-all-time determination of the nature of things, is for Nancy no longer an option, and maybe was always in error; nor for him will a Last Judgement reveal what was up until that closure of time seen only through a glass darkly. In *The Creation of the World*, Nancy also expresses doubts about the viability of the term 'biopower', as taken up by admirers of Michel Foucault. This connects back to a question posed by him to the term 'political technology' in his earlier *The Experience of Freedom*, in which he reads Heidegger on freedom as, at base, not a characteristic of human beings, but as a feature of ontological opening, making possible an arrival of self-affirming and self-destructive individuals. He appears there to find more in common with Jacques Rancière, with Jean-Francois Lyotard and indeed with Hannah Arendt, than with either Foucault or Heidegger.

For Nancy, democracy is not a given form of government, with a fixed meaning, but a term whose meaning is in contestation, always in process of reconfiguration and of arriving (*a-venir*). It does not provide a given standard by which to measure current relations and conditions. Nor is his thinking utopian in the sense of envisaging a new improved order: there is only a here and now, with its dynamic of a given order, claiming sovereignty, and a correlative potential for an insurrection of as yet unconfigured forces. An essence (*Wesen*) of being as oscillation between arrival and departure (*Anwesen* and *Abwesen*) is displaced in favour of a notion of a contingent being in common. With Rancière, Nancy has in common a notion of a *partage,* a sharing or distribution of meaning and sensibility; with Lyotard, he shares a sensitivity to a demand for sense, arriving in the absence of given significations, and a preoccupation with figures of a Last Judgment, a day of wrath, in which first and last things (*res ipsa et ultima*) arrive in order. His paper in honour of Lyotard from 1982, recently published in English translation as *Dies Irae* (2019, 1982), day of wrath, day of judgement, concludes: 'in this genesis, there is no day of rest'. Nancy is sceptical about both a secularisation thesis, whereby political community is supposed to arrive in an emptied-out space of collective religious observance, and about Carl Schmitt's hypothesis concerning a relocation of theological concepts, as concepts of and for the political. Each separates out religion from theology, in a way characteristic of Christianity, and then seeks to re-deploy one or other, without taking into account the full force of a European inheritance – monolithic, imperial, colonising and anti-Semitic. so many people have suffered Lacoue-Labarthe and Nancy organised the first of the major conferences addressing Derrida's thought at Cerisy la Salle in 1980,'The Ends of Man: Concerning the Work of Jacques Derrida', to which Nancy also contributed his essay 'The Free Voice of Humanity'. The first joint publication by Lacoue-Labarthe and Nancy, *The Title of the Letter: A Reading of Lacan* (1992, 1973), has the distinction of being recommended by both Jacques Lacan, in *Seminar XX: Encore: on Feminine Sexuality, the Limits of Love and Knowledge, 1972–1973* (1998, 1975), and by Jacques Derrida, in a footnote to *The Post Card: From Socrates to Freud and Beyond* (1987, 1980). The second joint publication, *The Literary Absolute: The Theory of Literature in German Romanticism* (1988, 1978) sets out a third term, circumscribing a commonality of themes: philosophy, psychoanalysis and literature, to which might be added a fourth: the politics of translation, in the first instance from German into French, and then of everything into English. The conference proceedings for *The Ends of Man* might be thought to be their third joint publication. In due course, Derrida invented for each a term to capture the distinctive gestures of their thought. The term *désistance* marks Lacoue-Labarthe's respect for what does not give itself for inspection, and is developed by Derrida in an introduction to the English translation of *Typography: Mimesis, Philosophy, Politics* (1989). For Nancy, the term is *le toucher*, ambiguously 'the touch', 'touching him' or 'touching it', in *On Touching—Jean-Luc Nancy* (2005, 2000). This citation from Nancy's brief foreword conjoins three terms important for his analyses: sense, absence, exposition. Derrida approaches his thinking through an elaboration of a notion of tangents, a circumscription without framing, exploring a distinctively French reception of Husserl's phenomenology, with its emphasis on a difference between inanimate bodies (*Koerper*) and lived flesh (*Leib*), from Merleau-Ponty and Levinas, to the Christian phenomenologists, Didier Franck and Jean-Louis Chretien. Derrida there interrupts himself to remark that this touch is both that of this phenomenological reception, and for Nancy, in addition, that of a self-dividing voice, resulting from processes of hearing oneself speak, and of a writing on skin, the *expeausition* and *excription*, as explored by Nancy in *Corpus* (2008, 1992) and *The Sense of the World* (1997,1993).

In an early essay, 'The Sublime Offering' (1993, 1988), Nancy explores the claim: 'What is at stake in the sublime is a suspension of art, a placing in question of art within art itself, as work or as task.' This he does by placing alongside each other texts by Benjamin and Heidegger, Adorno and Kant, Bataille and Blanchot, seeking out the nature of an art expressive of anguish as much as one expressive of joy. He finds them inseparably touching on one another: 'The beautiful and the sublime, if they are not identical – and indeed quite the contrary – take place on the same site, and in a certain sense the one upon the other, the one along the edge of the other and perhaps ... the one through the other.' He concludes a later essay, 'Strange Foreign Bodies' (2013, 2009), in *Corpus II: Writings on Sexuality* (2013): 'Still it is not that "art" domesticates and thereby reduces the strangeness of the body. On the contrary, it exposes it and deepens or accentuates it, exaggerates it if need be, aggravates it, tracks it down only in order to let it escape. It opens for it the space of limitless expansion.' This essay reproduces the script of a short film, *Outlandish: Strange Foreign Bodies*: part of a joint program of work with the film maker Phillip Wallard. *Corpus*, now the title of two collections of Nancy's writings in English published in 2008 and 2013, is a theme through which are conjoined three of Nancy's central concerns: the legacy of Christianity; the affirmations of embodiment in phenomenology and of sexuality in psychoanalysis; and an infinite expansion of bodies in artistic practices of all kinds. To these should be added his preoccupation with the dismemberment of the body politic in the various crises of nation and state.

The reception of Jean-Luc Nancy's writings in the Anglo-American world began with translations of the joint work with Lacoue-Labarthe, which then extended into the discussions of a *retrait* of politics, a retracing and withdrawal of politics, associated with their *Centre de recherches philosophiques sur la politique* (1980-1984). Some of this discussion arrived in English in *Retreating the Political* (1997), edited by Simon Sparks. Explorations under way there underpin both the hypothesis of an unworking of community, and the extended discussion by Nancy, in *The Experience of Freedom*, of the fate of concepts of freedom, and indirectly of politics, in the volatile conditions of the second half of the twentieth century. Two collections of papers edited by Nancy in the late eighties appeared in English translation, in the early nineties: *Who Comes after the Subject?* (1991, 1988), questioning the structure of question and response, and *Of the Sublime: Presence in Question* (1993, 1988), in which the essay 'The Sublime Offering' is to be found. In *Who Comes After the Subject?*, there appears a complete version of the interview, 'Eating well: or the calculation of the subject, an interview with Jacques Derrida', conducted by Nancy. Nancy there boldly states: 'For Heidegger, nevertheless, the epoch that comes to a close as the epoch of metaphysics, and that perhaps closes epochality as such, is the epoch of the metaphysics of subjectivity, and the end of philosophy is then the exiting of the metaphysics of subjectivity.' In their juxtaposition, these collections explore connections between concepts of subjectivity and sublimity, in art and in politics, revealing a metaphysical complicity, which extends to concepts of sovereignty and substance.

Alongside the joint work with Lacoue-Labarthe, Nancy published responses to Hegel, Kant and Descartes, which have been translated as *The Speculative Remark*

(One of Hegel's Bons Mots) (2001, 1973) by Céline Surprénant, as *The Discourse of the Syncope: Logodaedalus* (2008, 1976) by Saul Anton, and as *Ego Sum: Corpus, Anima, Fabula* (2016, 1979) by Marie-Eve Morin. The translators remark both the difficulty of the enterprise and the generous participation of their initiator. These texts have proved difficult to respond to, no less in French than in English, as a consequence of a very distinctively dense style of close reading practiced in them. Starting with *The Experience of Freedom*, Nancy adopted and adapted a mode of writing in juxtaposed fragments, which, while freighted with references to the tradition, and with many invocations of current discussions, provide interruptions in which to pause and consider what has taken place on the page. The sensation of towering heights of learning is curiously at variance with the tone of approachable conviviality, notable in the many interviews Nancy encouraged his readers to conduct with him, including in the most recent and now posthumously published conversations, from Duke University Press, *The Deconstruction of Sex*. Some thinkers may die already in their own lifetimes. Jean-Luc Nancy is revered in memory and, as author, living on in the modes of recent, and imminent publications.

Joanna Hodge is Professor Emerita in Philosophy: Aesthetics, Critique, History, at Manchester Metropolitan University, and author of The Singular Politics of Jean-Luc Nancy, *forthcoming with Bloomsbury.*

www.ingramcontent.com/pod-product-compliance
Lightning Source LLC
Chambersburg PA
CBHW050716090526

44588CB00015B/2341